Cars of the World in Colour

PASSENGER CARS
1924-1942

by
MICHAEL SEDGWICK

Illustrated by
JOHN W. WOOD

BLANDFORD PRESS

First published in 1975
by Blandford Press Ltd,
167 High Holborn, London WCIV 6PH

© Blandford Press Ltd 1975

ISBN 0 7137 0657 0

Colour illustrations printed by Colour Reproductions, Billericay
Text printed and books bound by Cox & Wyman Ltd, Fakenham

ACKNOWLEDGEMENTS

The author wishes to thank the following for their generous assistance in the compilation of this book:

In the United Kingdom: John Davy
Harry Edwards
G. N. Georgano
M. E. N. Moody
Brian E. Smith
Bart H. Vanderveen
Jonathan Wood
Peter Woodend
Allan N. Wright

In Australia: Edward du Cros
In Belgium: Ivan Mahy
In Czechoslovakia: Marian Suman-Hreblay
In France: Paul Badré
In Germany: Hans Heinrich von Fersen
Albert Leonhard
Hans Mai
Halwart Schrader

In Hungary: Lajos Haris
In Italy: Giancarlo Amari
Angelo Tito Anselmi

In New Zealand: Maurice D. Hendry
In Sweden: Björn-Eric Lindh
In the USA: Alfred S. Lewerenz
Keith Marvin
Charles Weaver

In the USSR: M. H. Kuuse

INTRODUCTION

Cynics have dismissed the 1924-42 period as one in which the craftsman withered and died, and the cost-accountant took over. Magnetos were supplanted by coils; nickel plate and paint-and-varnish by chromium and cellulose (Duco). Side-opening hoods gave way to caves guarded by the jaws of a metallic alligator, and in lieu of functional shapes came something called *Styling*, which tidied filler caps, headlamps and spare wheels away out of sight, and made plastic umbrella-handles out of handbrake levers. If no European manufacturer as yet approached Henry Ford's achievement of a million identical Model Ts in a year, firms of the calibre of Opel or Morris were good for six-figure outputs. Modestly-priced, 'different' species like the Italian Bianchi (14) or the French La Licorne (28) had either vanished, or had ceased to be different. Even the use of semi-custom bodies, essayed by companies like Hillman or Rover in the early thirties to 'pad' a range, was being frustrated by the spread of unitary construction.

Much of this is fair. In Europe, the magneto was still in use in 1929, on cars such as Swift (27) and Salmson (33). Nine years later its application was confined to out-and-out sporting machinery, even Rolls-Royce having switched to twin coils. 'Indestructible' Duco finish, pioneered in 1924 on the American Oakland (2), was universal by 1931, and though fanatics such as

Gabriel Voisin might inveigh against the meretriciousness of chromium plate, even Voisin was using it in 1935. To be fair, of course, he and the other traditionalists refrained from such excesses as those of the Buick (57). The alligator hood had arrived with a vengeance on De Soto (52) and Lincoln-Zephyr (58), but four years later it had been adapted to the 10 h.p. sedans of Austin and Hillman (78). Lesser makes were losing their individuality: Berliet were using Peugeot bodies, Chenard-Walckers were an untidy *mélange* of Ford and Citroën components, Bianchis looked like last year's Fiats, and something with the respected name of Sunbeam-Talbot was in fact a Hillman or a Humber (according to size) in a somewhat tawdry party frock. As for unitary construction, what Lancia (51) had pioneered in 1922 was now catching on in a big way, the merits of low cost-per-copy and structural strength outweighing the disadvantages (a need for long production runs, and an acute rust-proneness that militated against a gracious old age). Opel (62) and Citroën (74) were among the European leaders, backed by Hillman, Morris and Vauxhall. This assisted the spread of the American doctrine of planned obsolescence.

As for styling, this had taken over in the USA from the moment that Harley Earl created his La Salle (45) in 1927. The classical, Hispano-Suiza line lasted until the f.w.d. Cord of 1929 bred a new school, based on low build and elongated hoods, cleverly adapted by Chrysler to their 1931 models (36). Next came the skirted fenders and compound curves of the 1932 Graham (44), before General Motors again took the lead with their 1934 La Salle (45); its contributions included pontoon fenders, a narrow grille, and 'turret top' body. By 1938 Cadillac's Sixty Special (66) had gathered all the sheet metal elements into a harmonious whole: the boot blended into the main body, running-boards and traditional radiator were eliminated, pillars were thin, and filler caps concealed. Even the sacred dual sidemounts were sacrificed, though the steering-column gearchange was a form of obsessive tidiness that mercifully lasted only a quarter of a century.

The disease, of course, spread to Europe, where the sporting S.S. represents the apotheosis of the Cord theme. Traces of it can still be found in the Aero (69). Volvo tried their luck with Chrysler's abortive Airflow shape (52), and the 1937 Renault (65) stands as an awful warning of what can be achieved by using second-hand ideas from Detroit.

On the credit side, however, the automobile was made fool-proof and better suited to an uncritical laity, as yet uninfluenced by the outpourings of sophisticated motoring journalists. Angry home mechanics who delved in the dark caverns of an Airflow's hood could comfort themselves that maintenance schedules, constant decarbonisings and rebores were on their way out, replaced by cheap exchange units and flat-rate servicing, the secret of the Chevrolet's (79) success. Even Tatra (55) used a quick-detachable power pack on their rear-engined vee-eight. Other aids to easy maintenance were one-shot lubrication, general on better-class cars of the thirties and permanent jacks, found on Stars (38) in 1932, though the power tyre pumps of the Dagmar (1) and Farman (6) vanished in the middle twenties.

To assess the extent of progress, one should contemplate the 1924 Bean (4), a typical British family car of its era.

Bean 14 chassis 1924

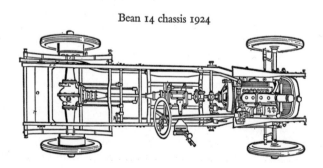

Of styling there was none, and the only real advances on 1914 technique were the full electrics, the detachable cylinder head, and the (optional extra) front-wheel brakes. It could carry five people at a steady 40–45 m.p.h., but close on 2½ litres were required to produce a modest 32 b.h.p. A slow-turning engine discouraged 'driving on the gears', even if double-declutching presented no terrors to its owner. The steering would have daunted his wife, suspension was hard, and a gallon of petrol lasted twenty miles. The paint-and-varnish finish required regular attention, preferably after each journey.

Of about the same litreage was the 1938 Peugeot (68). Its four-wheel brakes, synchromesh and cellulose paintwork went without saying, as (on the Continent, if not in Britain) did its independently-sprung front wheels. The advantages of good aerodynamics, a wider rev.-band, and twice the Bean's b.h.p., added up to a cruising speed of 60–65 m.p.h. and better fuel economy. Not everyone, however, wanted the Peugeot's eight seats, and smaller families could have attained mile-a-minute speeds and 35 m.p.g. (not to mention the Bean's 32 brake horses) with a 1,089 cc Skoda (70).

Nowhere were these basic trends so apparent as in America, still the world's general provider. Not that Detroit moved away from a stereotype—design in fact grew more uniform after the Great Depression; but the norm changed.

Some factors were, of course, con-stant, in 1942 as in 1924. Among these were side valves, three forward speeds, coil ignition, single-plate clut-ches, semi-elliptic rear springs, and spiral bevel back axles, though the hypoid rear end with its lower line was adopted by Packard (19) in 1927, followed in 1929 by Pierce-Arrow (32), and by a large section of the industry by the later thirties.

Other changes were undramatic. Vacuum fuel feed was common practice in 1924, but seven years later the mechanical pump predominated. Electric pumps, an American innova-tion, were used there only briefly in the middle and late twenties; they were more popular in Britain, where they were adopted by Rover (54) and Morris (60).

In 1924 American opinion was still divided over the merits of front-wheel brakes, though at least Americans were spared the uncoupled arrangements of Imperia (25) and B.M.W.-Dixi, *alias* Baby Austin (34). Of the volume-producers, Buick, Chrysler and Packard were quick off the mark, though the expanding type was not in general use until 1930, Studebaker's cheap Erskine of 1927 (18) being an early exception. Though Duesenberg had offered hydraulics in 1921, and Chrysler three years later, these were still mistrusted, and of eighteen makes using them in 1929 only four (Chrysler and its asso-ciates) were in the big league. By 1938 only Ford still held out, and Ford was soon to fall into line. An unpleasing adjunct of early hydraulics on both

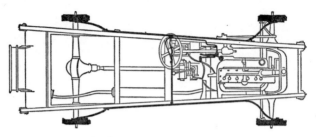

Hydraulic brake layout 1920s

sides of the Atlantic was the transmission handbrake, still standard on Chrysler products in 1942; it was retained by Fiat (63) until the early sixties.

O.H.V. gained no further American recruits, despite its spread in Europe: 1924's old stalwarts, Buick, Chevrolet and Nash, were still alone in 1942. Multi-cylinderism, however, was rampant. As late as 1928 all the cheap volume-seller were fours, and Overland had but recently introduced their Whippet (15). The Chevrolet, however, became a six in 1929, and three years later Ford (43) came out with a cut-price V8. Otherwise sixes tended to be the norm in the under $1,000 (£200) class, with straight-eights on the march in higher price categories, though Marmon's Roosevelt of 1929 (26) offered such a configuration at a new, low price, resoundingly beaten by Pontiac's $585 effort of 1933. Before sound insulation and softer suspensions took over, there was a brief craze for multi-barrelled engines which unfortunately coincided with the Depression.

In 1932 America offered six different V-12s, among them the air-cooled Franklin (50), not to mention a brace of V-16s. The pure delight of feeling no power impulses at all palled somewhat when the fuel bills came in! First of the European twelves was, of course, the monstrous and complicated Daimler of 1927 (20).

Chassis grew stiffer: the 1929 Cord's cruciform bracing was generally copied, and of necessity, as owners of 1932 Ford V-8s rapidly found out. Though Chrysler-De Soto (52), Lincoln (58) and Nash (80) tried various forms of unitary construction, the principle found little favour in the New World. American suspensions were aimed at a 'boulevard ride'; what hydraulic dampers failed to achieve in the twenties was attempted with a diversity of i.f.s. systems, from Hudson's divided axle to G.M.'s Dubonnet coils. Most of them combined smooth passage over washboard roads with the worst possible kind of non-handling. Buick and Nash were among those who tried a live axle and coils at the rear, but by 1940 only Ford

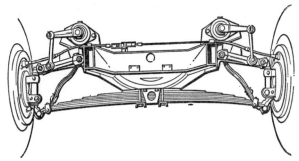

Transverse-leaf independent front suspension mid 1930s

remained obstinately loyal to beam axles at both ends. In the light of this it is remarkable to note that only in the USA did the fixed road wheel survive into our period. Wood wheels and demountable rims persisted until 1931, on the principle that they were lighter for a woman to change. The wire wheel disappeared after 1935 because it was tiresome to clean.

Essex had paved the way with cheap closed cars in 1922, and seven years later closed bodies accounted for 90 per cent of sales. Along with styling came full-size integral boots, no-draught ventilation (a 1933 fad), heaters, defrosters, and seats convertible into a bed (found also on the 1924 Dagmar!). 1931 Chryslers were wired for radio. The 'sliding roof', universal on British sedans of the thirties, let in too much dust for comfort, and interfered with American presswork techniques. A logical replacement for the roadster was the convertible coupe, which became common around 1927; curi-ously, Americans clung until 1937 to the discriminatory rumble seat, replaced by an uncomfortable sideways-facing single 'opera seat', and finally by full five-seater styles, some of which had acquired power tops by 1940. More important still was the dual-purpose station wagon, austere within, and half-timbered without. Sales were still modest, but a firm as important as Chevrolet (79) deemed it desirable to offer a wagon in 1941.

Gear-changing—or its avoidance—always engaged Detroit's attention, though it was left to Maybach of Germany (13) to perpetuate Ford's two-speed pedal-controlled transmission. The first steps towards painless shifting came in 1929, with Cadillac's synchromesh, adopted by the rest of the industry within a couple of years. Some makers, notably Chrysler, Graham-Paige, Packard and Pierce- Arrow, tried 'dual-range' four-speed boxes, but these were not a success, and Chrysler's automatic overdrive of 1934

9

proved a better way of achieving a high cruising gear. Auburn and Franklin used two-speed back axles, also found in Europe in the shape of the Maybach and Cotal systems; Berliet (23) fitted the latter.

Though semi-automatics came early to America, with Reo's 'self-shifter'

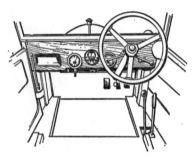

Clyno dashboard 1926

Typical American Dashboard 1937

(1933), Hudson's Electric Hand (1935), and the four-speed affair offered by Buick and Oldsmobile in 1938, they were neither clutchless nor as successful as European preselectors, pioneered by two British firms, Armstrong Siddeley (1928) and Daimler (1930), and found on the luxury Autovia (64) launched by Riley in 1936. France's electrically-

selected Cotal was probably better still, and though it was usually found on sports cars, Salmson (33) applied it too. Since Americans seldom used first gear, they did not bother to synchronise it; thus to Alvis of Great Britain (1934) goes the credit of the first all-synchromesh box to see series production. Hillmans and Humbers had it a year later. Automatics as such did not come until the end of our period, the simple two-speed Hydramatic being an option on 1940 Oldsmobiles, and on Cadillacs a year later.

The American idiom, of course, spread into Europe, with a wave of multi-cylindered stereotypes introduced between 1927 and 1932. Few people paused to consider that a European factory could not sell enough cars to render such ideas economic, but typical of such thinking were Sweden's Volvo (31) and Hungary's Magosix (30). These two prospered because they were the only native marques available. As for straight-eights, these proliferated, especially in Germany, where the Stoewer (24) was typical. They were even less successful than the sixes.

But if fiscal problems killed off such big eights as the Beverley-Barnes (10), there was that unhappy *mariage de convenance* between flexibility and the tax-man known as the pint-sized six, which did everything an American automobile could do at the price of valve bounce at 55 m.p.h. Some, like the Czechoslovak Praga (29) and Renault's Monasix, were merely solid and gutless, but low comedy is represented by the 'instant sixes' evolved by taking a baby-car chassis and lengthening (but seldom strengthening) it sufficiently to take two extra cylinders. The 1931 Triumph (39) from Coventry is a copy-book example of the disease, but it was neither British-born nor Depression-bred; Mathis (7) was doing it in France as early as 1923.

Outside America, of course, regional considerations obtained, and most cars were designed with home-market customers in view. Britain had a horsepower tax based on cylinder bore alone, which inhibited engine development. Japan's Automobile Control Law laid down strict regulations on size and capacity, while the combination of appalling roads and a bellicose government produced near-dead-ends such as the Datsun (56). Czechoslovakia protected her small industry so jealously that it had to cover every sector of the market; in 1935 her eight manufacturers offered everything from two-stroke twins to Tatra's vast 6-litre V-12. As for the Soviet Union, cars were a badge of rank or concomitants to somebody's job; thus rugged imitations of obsolescent American themes like the ZIS (77) sufficed. Odd loopholes in the law ensured cyclecar-survivals, even if France abandoned her famous 350-kilogram category after 1925, leaving such oddities as the Sima-Violet (8) to linger awhile. In pre-Hitler days, however, Germany offered special concessions to minicars of under 200 cc, with consequence that things like the Goliath (48) enjoyed a brief vogue. Britain allowed certain concessions to three-wheelers, which were 'honorary motor-cycles' until 1935, but once these concessions were swept away, the market died, killing the J.M.B. (53), the Raleigh, and the B.S.A.; only the sporting Morgan survived.

Only where exports bulked large was progress rampant, and not always then. Austria's Steyr (17) survived the

Fiat 508C chassis 1938

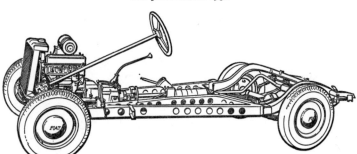

holocaust thanks to a local, Central European market, but Belgium's industry committed *hara-kiri*, ably assisted by a Government which admitted the Americans and their assembly plants in 1926. If Imperia and F.N. (35) at least tried to satisfy the home market with modest sedans, Minerva (49) stayed with the vast sleeve-valve carriages once beloved of wealthy Britons, and died of it.

Thus for real technical progress the world relied on Germany and Italy. The Germans at long last snapped out of the apathy that had bred antiques like the 1924 N.A.G. (8), and the pseudo-Americans of Adler, Hansa and Stoewer. Foreign exchange was desperately needed, and foreign exchange meant exports. Spurred on by the restless journalist Josef Ganz, German makers cast away all the shibboleths of the *système* Panhard. Not for them the complacent ways of Britain, where the public would have to wait until 1939 for i.f.s. on a cheap baby car, the

Standard (72). All-independent springing featured on Röhr, D.K.W. (40), Mercedes-Benz (61), and Horch (75), among others. By 1933, not only D.K.W., but Adler, Audi and Stoewer had f.w.d. models in series production. The rear engine's chief protagonist was Hans Ledwinka of the Czechoslovak Tatra firm (55), but as early as 1925 the little Hanomag (12) had enjoyed quite a following, and nearly 10,000 of Mercedes-Benz' unsuccessful *heckmotor* were sold between 1933 and 1938. It was left to the daemon of Hitler and the ingenuity of Ferdinand Porsche to carry ideas to their logical conclusion on the Volkswagen (76), in which the ingredient of frost-proof air cooling was added to produce a true people's car to replace the Model-T Ford, even if fifteen years were to elapse before the Beetle made its mark. Italy was even more export-oriented, poorer than her Axis ally, and afflicted with a small home market which Fiat alone could have satisfied without working a single

Citroën 7CV unitary construction, 1934

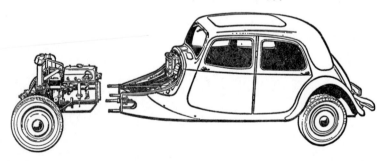

hour's overtime. Fiat, it is true, made their mistakes, notably the 514 of 1929, but their mock-Americans were better made than most. The 508 of 1932 was built under licence in four foreign countries, and they scored two big hits with the miniature 500 (63) and its bigger sister the 1100 of 1937: both with hydraulic brakes, i.f.s., up-to-the-minute styling, and an excellent mixture of performance, handling, and frugality.

If Britain's main contribution continued to be such beautifully-made luxury models as the Rolls-Royce (5), France was bedevilled by industrial unrest, antiquated factories, and national conservatism. The 'ebullient decade' of the twenties produced splendid luxury cars like the Hispano-Suiza and the Farman, not to mention middle-class tourers such as the Hotchkiss (21), but the thirties were depressing. Panhard (47) produced excellent vehicles on antiquated lines. Citroën (74) was the honourable exception to a sad rule, with the brilliant unitary-construction, f.w.d. line introduced in 1934. This, along with Germany's B.M.W., and the Fiat 1100 and Lancia Aprilia from Italy, marked the shape of things to come in Europe.

THE COLOUR PLATES

1
Dagmar 24–6–80, 1924, U.S.A. Water-cooled, six vertical cylinders in line. 95.2×139.7mm, 5940cc. Coil ignition. Four forward speeds. Spiral bevel drive. Half-elliptic springs front and rear.

2

Oakland 6–54, 1924, U.S.A. Water-cooled, six vertical cylinders in line. 71.4×120.7mm, 2899cc. Side valves. Coil ignition. Three forward speeds. Spiral bevel drive. Half-elliptic springs front and rear.

3
Bean Fourteen, 1924 (bottom), 1925 (top), Great Britain. Water-cooled, four vertical cylinders in line. 75×135mm, 2385cc. Side valves. High-tension magneto ignition. Four forward speeds. Spiral bevel drive. Half-elliptic springs front and rear.

4

Jowett Long Four, 1924, Great Britain. Water-cooled, two horizontally opposed cylinders. 75.4×101.6mm, 907cc. Side valves. Coil ignition. Three forward speeds. Spiral bevel drive. Half-elliptic springs front and rear.

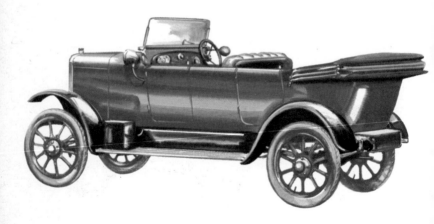

5

Rolls-Royce Twenty, 1924 (top), 1926 (bottom), Great Britain. Water-cooled, six vertical cylinders in line. 76.2×114.3mm, 3127cc. Top, coil ignition, bottom, high-tension magneto and coil ignition. Top, three forward speeds, bottom, four forward speeds. Spiral bevel drive. Half-elliptic springs front and rear.

6

Farman A6B 40CV, 1924, France. Water-cooled, six vertical cylinders in line. 100×140mm, 6597cc. Overhead camshaft. High-tension magneto and coil ignition. Four forward speeds. Spiral bevel drive. Front, half-elliptic springs, rear, cantilever springs.

7

Mathis PS 10CV, 1924, France. Water-cooled, six vertical cylinders in line. 55×80mm, 1140cc. Side valves. High-tension magneto ignition. Four forward speeds. Spiral bevel drive. Half-elliptic springs front and rear.

8

N.A.G. D4, 1924, Germany. Water-cooled, four vertical cylinders in line. 78×136mm, 2599cc. Overhead valves. High-tension magneto ignition. Four forward speeds. Spiral bevel drive. Half-elliptic springs front and rear.

9
Locomobile Junior Eight, 1925, U.S.A. Water-cooled, eight vertical cylinders in line. 71.4×101.6mm, 3254cc. Overhead valves. Coil ignition. Three forward speeds. Spiral bevel drive. Half-elliptic springs front and rear.

BEVERLEY-BARNES

10

Beverley-Barnes 24–80 h.p., 1925, Great Britain. Water-cooled, eight vertical cylinders in line. 75×112mm, 3994cc. Overhead camshaft. High-tension magneto ignition. Three forward speeds. Spiral bevel drive. Half-elliptic springs front and rear.

11
Sima-Violet, 1925, France. Air-cooled, two horizontally opposed cylinders. 65×75mm, 496cc. Two-stroke. High-tension magneto ignitipn. Two forward speeds. Shaft and bevel drive. Front, transverse spring, rear, quarter-elliptic springs.

HANOMAG

12

Hanomag 'Kommissbrot' 2/10PS, 1925, Germany. Water-cooled, single vertical cylinder. 80×100mm, 499cc. Overhead valves. High-tension magneto ignition. Three forward speeds. Chain drive. Front, transverse spring, rear, coil springs.

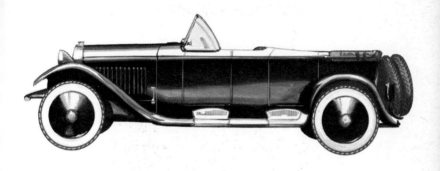

13

Maybach W3, 1925 (top), W5, 1927 (bottom), Germany. Water-cooled, six vertical cylinders in line. Top, 95×135mm, 5741cc, bottom, 94×168mm, 6996cc. Top, side valves, bottom, overhead valves. High-tension magneto and coil ignition. Two forward speeds. Spiral bevel drive. Half-elliptic springs front and rear.

14

Bianchi S4, 1925, Italy. Water-cooled, four vertical cylinders in line. 64 × 100mm, 1287cc. Overhead valves. High-tension magneto ignition. Four forward speeds. Spiral bevel drive. Half-elliptic springs front and rear.

15
Overland Whippet Four, 1926, U.S.A. Water-cooled, four vertical cylinders in line. 79.4×111.1mm, 2199cc. Side valves. Coil ignition. Three forward speeds. Spiral bevel drive. Half-elliptic springs front and rear.

16
Clyno 10.8 h.p., 1926 (bottom), 1927 (top), Great Britain. Water-cooled, four vertical cylinders in line. 66×100mm, 1368cc. Side valves. High-tension magneto ignition. Three forward speeds. Spiral bevel drive. Front, half-elliptic springs, rear, quarter-elliptic springs.

17

Steyr Type XII, 1926, Austria. Water-cooled, six vertical cylinders in line. 61.5×88mm, 1560cc. Overhead camshaft. Coil ignition. Four forward speeds. Spiral bevel drive. Front, half-elliptic springs, rear, independent coil springs and swing axles.

18

Erskine Six, 1927, U.S.A. Water-cooled, six vertical cylinders in line. 66.7×
114.3mm, 2394cc. Side valves. Coil ignition. Three forward speeds. Spiral
bevel drive. Half-elliptic springs front and rear.

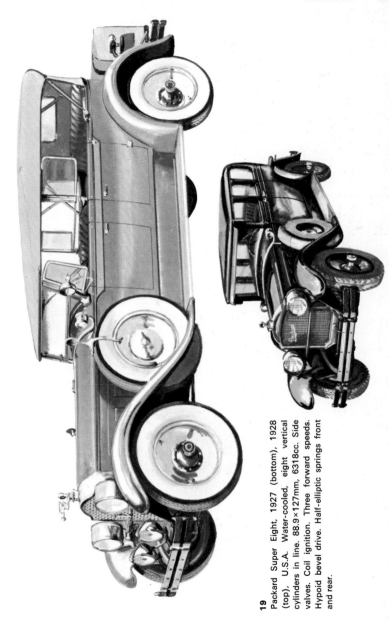

19
Packard Super Eight, 1927 (bottom), 1928 (top). U.S.A. Water-cooled, eight vertical cylinders in line. 88.9×127mm, 6318cc. Side valves. Coil ignition. Three forward speeds. Hypoid bevel drive. Half-elliptic springs front and rear.

20
Daimler Double-Six-50, 1927 (bottom), 1929 (top). Great Britain. Water-cooled, twelve cylinders in vee formation. 81.5 × 114mm, 7136cc. Double sleeve valves. Ignition by twin high-tension magnetos and twin coils. Four forward speeds. Shaft and worm drive. Half-elliptic springs front and rear.

21

Hotchkiss AM2 12CV, 1927 (top), 1930 (bottom), France. Water-cooled, four vertical cylinders in line. 80×120mm, 2412cc. Overhead valves. High-tension magneto ignition. Four forward speeds. Spiral bevel drive. Half-elliptic springs front and rear.

SINGER

22
Singer Junior, 1928 (top), 1930 (bottom), Great Britain. Water-cooled, four vertical cylinders in line. 56×86mm, 848cc. Overhead camshaft. Top, high-tension magneto ignition, bottom, coil ignition. Three forward speeds. Spiral bevel drive. Top, front: half-elliptic springs, rear: quarter-elliptic springs; bottom, half-elliptic springs front and rear.

23
Berliet 11CV, 1928, France. Water-cooled, six vertical cylinders in line.
65×100mm, 1991cc. Side valves. Coil ignition. Four forward speeds. Spiral
bevel drive. Half-elliptic springs front and rear.

STOEWER

24

Stoewer S10 Superior, 1928 (bottom), G15 Gigant, 1930 (top), Germany. Water-cooled, eight vertical cylinders in line. Bottom, 62×102mm, 2462cc, top, 72×122mm, 3974cc. Side valves. Coil ignition. Four forward speeds. Spiral bevel drive. Half-elliptic springs front and rear.

25

Imperia 6CV, 1928 (top), 1930 (bottom), Belgium. Water-cooled, four vertical cylinders in line. 66×80mm, 1094cc. Side valves. Top, high-tension magneto ignition, bottom, coil ignition. Four forward speeds. Spiral bevel drive. Half-elliptic springs front and rear.

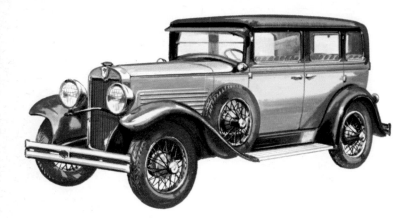

26
Roosevelt, 1929, U.S.A. Water-cooled, eight vertical cylinders in line. 69.8×
114.3mm, 3310cc. Side valves. Coil ignition. Three forward speeds. Hypoid
bevel drive. Half-elliptic springs front and rear.

27
Swift 10 h.p., 1929, Great Britain. Water-cooled, four vertical cylinders in line. 62.5×97mm, 1190cc. Side valves. High-tension magneto ignition. Four forward speeds. Spiral bevel drive. Half-elliptic springs front and rear.

LA LICORNE

28

La Licorne 5CV, 1929 (top), 1930 (bottom), France. Water-cooled, four vertical cylinders in line. 60×80mm, 905cc. Side valves. High-tension magneto ignition. Three forward speeds. Spiral bevel drive. Front, half-elliptic springs, rear, quarter-elliptic springs.

29

Praga Alfa, 1929 (bottom), 1930 (top), Czechoslovakia. Water-cooled, six vertical cylinders in line. Bottom, 60×88mm, 1496cc, top, 65×90mm, 1792cc. Side valves. Coil ignition. Four forward speeds. Half-elliptic springs front and rear.

MAGOSIX

30
Magosix, 1929, Hungary. Water-cooled, six vertical cylinders in line, 72×100mm, 2443cc. Side valves. Coil ignition. Four forward speeds. Spiral bevel drive. Half-elliptic springs front and rear.

31
Volvo, PV651 1929 (top), PV653 1933 (bottom), Sweden. Water-cooled, six vertical cylinders in line. Top, 76.2×110mm, 3010cc, bottom, 79.4×110mm, 3266cc. Side valves. Coil ignition. Three forward speeds. Hypoid bevel drive. Half-elliptic springs front and rear.

32

Pierce-Arrow Eight, 1930, U.S.A. Water-cooled, eight vertical cylinders in line. 88.9×120.7mm, 5920cc. Side valves. Coil ignition. Three or four forward speeds. Hypoid bevel drive. Half-elliptic springs front and rear.

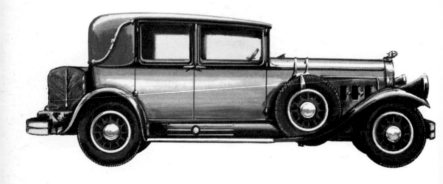

33

Salmson S4, 1930, France. Water-cooled, four vertical cylinders in line.
65×98mm, 1300cc. Twin overhead camshafts. High-tension magneto ignition.
Four forward speeds. Spiral bevel drive. Front, half-elliptic springs, rear,
quarter-elliptic springs.

B.M.W.

34

B.M.W. Dixi 3/15PS, 1930 (bottom), 1931 (top), Germany. Water-cooled, four vertical cylinders in line. 56×76mm, 747cc. Side valves. Coil ignition. Three forward speeds. Spiral bevel drive. Front, transverse spring, rear, quarter-elliptic springs.

35
F.N. 1625, 1930 (top), 1931 (bottom), Belgium. Water-cooled, four vertical cylinders in line. 72×100mm, 1628cc. Overhead valves. Coil ignition. Four forward speeds. Spiral bevel drive. Half-elliptic springs front and rear.

36
Chrysler CD, 1931, U.S.A. Water-cooled, eight vertical cylinders in line. 85.7×127mm, 4396cc. Side valves. Coil ignition. Four forward speeds. Spiral bevel drive. Half-elliptic springs front and rear.

37

De Vaux 6–75, 1931, U.S.A. Water-cooled, six vertical cylinders in line.
85.7×101.6mm, 3523cc. Side valves. Coil ignition. Three forward speeds.
Spiral bevel drive. Half-elliptic springs front and rear.

STAR COMET

38
Star Comet Eighteen, 1931 (top), 1932 (bottom), Great Britain. Water-cooled, six vertical cylinders in line. 69×110mm, 2470cc. Overhead valves. High-tension magneto ignition. Four forward speeds. Spiral bevel drive. Half-elliptic springs front and rear.

39
Triumph Scorpion, 1931 (top), 1932 (bottom), Great Britain. Water-cooled, six vertical cylinders in line. 56.5×80mm, 1203cc. Side valves. Coil ignition. Three forward speeds. Shaft and worm drive. Top, front, half-elliptic springs, rear, quarter-elliptic springs; bottom, half-elliptic springs front and rear.

D.K.W.

40

D.K.W. F1–500, 1931, Germany. Water-cooled, two vertical cylinders in line, transversely mounted. 68×68mm, 490cc. Two-stroke. Coil ignition. Three forward speeds. Spur gear drive to front wheels. Independent transverse springs front and rear.

41
Martini NF, 1931 (top), 1934 (bottom), Switzerland. Water-cooled, six vertical cylinders in line. 88×120mm, 4379cc. Side valves. High-tension magneto ignition. Four forward speeds. Shaft and worm drive. Half-elliptic springs front and rear.

42
Gräf *und* Stift SP8, 1931 (top), 1933 (bottom). Austria. Water-cooled, eight vertical cylinders in line. 85×132mm, 5923cc. Overhead camshaft. Coil ignition. Four forward speeds. Shaft and worm drive. Half-elliptic springs front and rear.

43
Ford V8 model-18, 1932, U.S.A. Water-cooled, eight cylinders in vee forma-
tion. 77.8×95.2mm, 3622cc. Side valves. Coil ignition. Three forward speeds.
Spiral bevel drive. Transverse springs front and rear.

GRAHAM

44
Graham Blue Streak, 1932 (bottom), Custom Supercharger Eight, 1934
(top), U.S.A. Water-cooled, eight vertical cylinders in line. Bottom, 79.4×
101.6mm, 4013cc, top, 82.55×114.3mm, 4350cc. Side valves. Coil ignition.
Three forward speeds. Sprial bevel drive. Half-elliptic springs front and rear.

45
La Salle, 1932 (bottom), 1934 (top and centre), U.S.A. Water-cooled, bottom, eight cylinders in vee formation, top and centre, eight vertical cylinders in line. Bottom, 85.4×125.4mm, 5784cc, top and centre, 76.2×107.95mm, 4187cc. Side valves. Coil ignition. Three forward speeds. Spiral bevel drive. Bottom, half-elliptic springs front and rear; top and centre, front, independent coil springs, rear, half-elliptic springs.

AUSTIN

46

Austin Ten-Four, 1932 (top), 1934 (bottom), Great Britain. Water-cooled, four vertical cylinders in line. 63.5×89mm, 1125cc. Side valves. Coil ignition. Four forward speeds. Spiral bevel drive. Half-elliptic springs front and rear.

47
Panhard 6CS 13CV, 1932, France. Water-cooled, six vertical cylinders in line.
69.5×103mm, 2300cc. Double sleeve valves. Coil ignition. Four forward
speeds. Spiral bevel drive. Half-elliptic springs front and rear.

GOLIATH

48
Goliath *Dreiradwagen*, 1932, Germany. Air-cooled, single horizontal cylinder. 63×64mm, 198cc. Two-stroke. Coil ignition. Three forward speeds. Shaft drive. Front, quarter-elliptic spring, rear, double quarter-elliptic springs.

49
Minerva AP 22CV, 1932 (bottom), 1934 (top),
Belgium. Water-cooled, eight vertical cylinders in
line. 75×112mm, 3994cc. Double sleeve valves.
Coil ignition. Four forward speeds. Spiral bevel
drive. Half-elliptic springs front and rear.

50

Franklin Series 17, 1933, U.S.A. Air-cooled twelve cylinders in vee formation. 82.5 × 102.5mm, 6585cc. Overhead valves. Coil ignition. Three forward speeds with two-speed rear axle. Spiral bevel drive. Half-elliptic springs front and rear.

51
Lancia Augusta, 1933 (top), 1935 (bottom), Italy. Water-cooled, four cylinders in vee formation. 69.85×78mm, 1194cc. Overhead camshaft. Coil ignition. Four forward speeds. Hypoid bevel drive. Front, independent coil springs, rear, half-elliptic springs.

52

De Soto Airflow SE, 1934, U.S.A. Water-cooled, six vertical cylinders in line. 85.7×114.3mm, 3956cc. Side valves. Coil ignition. Three forward speeds. Spiral bevel drive. Half-elliptic springs front and rear.

53
J.M.B., 1934 (top), 1935 (bottom), Great Britain. Air-cooled, single horizontal cylinder. 85.7×95mm, 497cc. Top, side valves, bottom, overhead valves. Coil ignition. Three forward speeds. Chain drive. Front, independent transverse springs, rear, cantilever spring.

54
Rover 14 h.p., 1935 (bottom), 1936 (top).
Great Britain. Water-cooled, six vertical
cylinders in line. 61×90mm, 1577cc.
Overhead valves. Coil ignition. Four
forward speeds. Spiral bevel drive. Half-
elliptic springs front and rear.

55
Tatra 77, 1935, Czechoslovakia. Air-cooled, eight cylinders in vee formation.
80×84mm, 3380cc (*see text*). Overhead valves. Coil ignition. Four forward
speeds. Spiral bevel drive. Front, independent transverse springs, rear,
independent coil springs.

DATSUN

56
Datsun, 1935 (top), 1937 (bottom), Japan. Water-cooled, four vertical cylinders in line. 55×76mm, 722cc. Side valves. Coil ignition. Three forward speeds. Shaft and worm drive. Front, transverse spring, rear, half-elliptic springs.

57
Buick Series-40, 1936, U.S.A. Water-cooled, eight vertical cylinders in line.
78.6×98.5mm, 3823cc. Overhead valves. Coil ignition. Three forward speeds.
Spiral bevel drive. Front, independent coil springs, rear, half-elliptic springs.

58

Lincoln-Zephyr, 1936 (top), 1937 (bottom), U.S.A. Water-cooled, twelve cylinders in vee formation. 69.8×95.2mm, 4387cc. Side valves. Coil ignition. Three forward speeds. Spiral bevel drive. Transverse springs front and rear.

59

Ford Ten, 1936 (bottom), 1938 (top), Great Britain. Water-cooled, four
vertical cylinders in line. 63.5×92.5mm, 1172cc. Side valves. Coil ignition.
Three forward speeds. Spiral bevel drive. Transverse springs front and rear.

60

Morris Twenty-Five Series II, 1936, Great Britain. Water-cooled, six vertical cylinders in line. 82×110mm, 3485cc. Side valves. Coil ignition. Three forward speeds. Spiral bevel drive. Half-elliptic springs front and rear.

61
Mercedes-Benz 170V, 1936, Germany. Water-cooled, four vertical cylinders
in line. 73.5×100mm, 1697cc. Side valves. Coil ignition. Four forward speeds.
Spiral bevel drive. Front, independent transverse springs, rear, independent coil
springs.

62

Opel P4, 1936, Germany. Water-cooled, four vertical cylinders in line. 67.5×75mm, 1074cc. Side valves. Coil ignition. Three forward speeds. Spiral bevel drive. Half-elliptic springs front and rear.

63

Fiat 500, 1936, Italy. Water-cooled, four vertical cylinders in line. 52×67mm, 569cc. Side valves. Coil ignition. Four forward speeds. Spiral bevel drive. Front, independent transverse springs, rear, quarter-elliptic springs.

64
Autovia 24 h.p., 1937, Great Britain. Water-cooled, eight cylinders in vee formation. 69×95.25mm, 2849cc. Overhead valves. High-tension magneto ignition. Four forward speeds. Shaft and worm drive. Half-elliptic springs front and rear.

65
Renault Celtaquatre 8CV, 1937, France. Water-cooled, four vertical cylinders in line. 70×95mm, 1463cc. Side valves. Coil ignition. Three forward speeds. Spiral bevel drive. Front, half-elliptic springs, rear, transverse spring.

CADILLAC

66

Cadillac Sixty Special, 1938, U.S.A. Water-cooled, eight cylinders in vee formation. 88.9 × 114.3mm, 5676cc. Side valves. Coil ignition. Three forward speeds. Hypoid bevel drive. Front, independent coil springs, rear, half-elliptic springs.

67
Humber Pullman, 1938, Great Britain. Water-cooled, six vertical cylinders in line. 85×120mm, 4086cc. Side valves. Coil ignition. Four forward speeds. Spiral bevel drive. Front, independent transverse springs, rear, half-elliptic springs.

68
Peugeot 402, 1938, France. Water-cooled, four vertical cylinders in line. 83×92mm, 1991cc. Over-head valves. Coil ignition. Three or four forward speeds. Shaft and worm drive. Front, independent transverse springs, rear, half-elliptic springs.

69

Aero A30 (top), A50 (bottom), 1938, Czechoslovakia. Water-cooled, (top) two, (bottom) four vertical cylinders in line. 85×88mm, (top) 998cc, (bottom) 1997cc. Two-stroke. Coil ignition. Three forward speeds. Spur gear drive to front wheels. Independent coil springs front and rear.

SKODA

70

Skoda Popular 1100, 1938, Czechoslovakia. Water-cooled, four vertical cylinders in line. 68×75mm, 1089cc. Overhead valves. Coil ignition. Four forward speeds. Spiral bevel drive. Front, independent transverse springs, rear, independent coil springs and swing axle.

71
Crosley, 1939 (top), 1940 (bottom), U.S.A. Air-cooled, two horizontally opposed cylinders. 76.2×69.8mm, 655cc. Side valves. Coil ignition. Three forward speeds. Spiral bevel drive. Front, half-elliptic springs, rear, quarter-elliptic springs.

STANDARD

72
Standard Flying 8, 1939, Great Britain. Water-cooled, four vertical cylinders in line. 57×100mm, 1021cc. Side valves. Coil ignition. Three forward speeds. Spiral bevel drive. Front, independent transverse springs, rear, half-elliptic springs.

73
Amilcar Compound B38, 1939, France. Water-cooled, four vertical cylinders in line. 63×95mm, 1185cc. Side valves. Coil ignition. Four forward speeds. Spiral bevel drive to front wheels. Front, independent transverse springs, rear, independent torsion bars.

74
Citroën 15CV, 1939, France. Water-cooled, six vertical cylinders in line. 78×100mm. 2866cc. Overhead valves. Coil ignition. Three forward speeds. Spiral bevel drive to front wheels. Front, independent torsion bars, rear, dead axle and torsion bars.

75

Horch 930, 1939, Germany. Water-cooled, eight cylinders in vee formation. 78×100mm, 3823cc. Side valves. Coil ignition. Four or five forward speeds. Shaft and worm drive. Front, independent transverse springs, rear, jointed axle and semi-elliptic springs (*see text*).

76

Volkswagen, 1939, Germany. Air-cooled, four horizontally opposed cylinders. 70×64mm, 985cc. Overhead valves. Coil ignition. Four forward speeds. Spiral bevel drive. Independent torsion bars front and rear.

77
ZIS-101, 1939, U.S.S.R. Water-cooled, eight vertical cylinders in line.
85×127mm, 5750cc. Overhead valves. Coil ignition. Three forward speeds.
Spiral bevel drive. Half-elliptic springs front and rear.

78

Hillman Minx, 1940, Great Britain. Water-cooled, four vertical cylinders in line. 63×95mm, 1185cc. Side valves. Coil ignition. Four forward speeds. Spiral bevel drive. Half-elliptic springs front and rear.

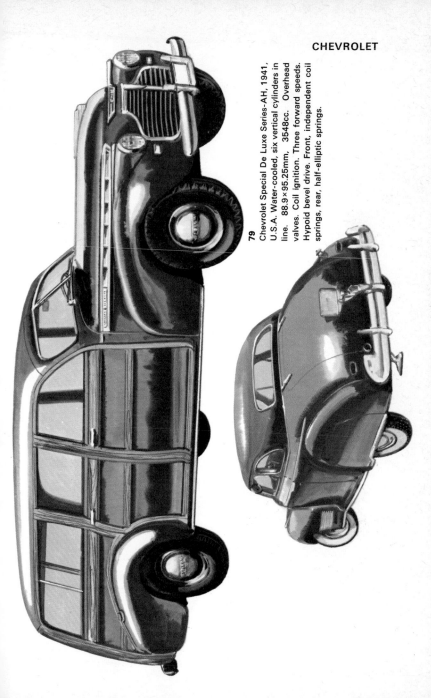

CHEVROLET

79

Chevrolet Special De Luxe Series-AH, 1941, U.S.A. Water-cooled, six vertical cylinders in line. 88.9×95.25mm, 3548cc. Overhead valves. Coil ignition. Three forward speeds. Hypoid bevel drive. Front, independent coil springs. rear, half-elliptic springs.

NASH

80
Nash 600, 1941 (top), 1942 (bottom), U.S.A. Water-cooled, six vertical cylinders in line. 79.4×95.2mm, 2827cc. Side valves. Coil ignition. Three forward speeds. Spiral bevel drive. Front, independent coil springs, rear, coil springs.

1 DAGMAR 24-6-80, 1924, USA

'The Car You Will Like Better at the Journey's End' was one of America's less usual assembled automobiles, even if the bits came from such recognized sources as Continental (engines), Brown-Lipe (transmissions), Gemmer (steering gears), and Timken (axles).

Its creator, Mathias Peter Möller, was a Dane whose Hagerstown, Maryland factory was America's most important producer of pipe organs. It was logical that he should back the local Crawford Bicycle Company's motor-car venture of 1904, and hardly surprising that fourteen years later he had bought out all the other shareholders. The Crawford was strictly orthodox: the same could not be said of the Dagmar, named (in the best Jellinek tradition) after Möller's daughter and launched in July 1922.

Its only mechanical heresy was the use of a four-speed gearbox with an overdrive top high enough to propel the car at more than 80 m.p.h., but the big 5·9-litre side-valve six-cylinder engine developed 80 b.h.p. at 2,400 r.p.m. The 138-inch wheelbase was an extravagance, since the only body offered until then was a close-coupled sporting phaeton with victoria top. No other weather protection was furnished, and the coachwork terminated ahead of the back axle, to leave space for a 35-gallon tank with foot-high filler.

Refinements included a swing-away 'fat man's' steering wheel and seats convertible into a double bed. The angular 'military fenders' (wings) were even more distinctive, while soupplate discs concealed ordinary fixed wood wheels. Tire-changing tools were concealed within the side-mounted 'spares'. The radiator aped the Packard's, and so did the hexagonal hubcaps which replaced the original conical type in 1924. Möller, however, could not afford Packard's anonymity, and used a badge which was a parody of the Danish Royal Arms. When his native land, understandably, objected, he switched to a pipe organ *motif.* Colour options were 'eggshell', 'chartreuse' or 'orchid', and radiators wore four-way Moto Meters, on which one face indicated the actual temperature; the others were red, green, and blue respectively. At $3,500 (£700), the Dagmar remained an object of discussion rather than a car to be bought, even after 1924's Miss America, Ruth Malcolmson, was presented with (and photographed in) a victoria-speedster.

By 1924, output was up to 80 b.h.p. and ordinary crown fenders had replaced the earlier type; the range included a six-window *'petite sedan'*, a brougham, and a coupe. A shorter-stroke Continental engine was used in 1925's big Dagmars. A smaller model was also tried, but production was falling away from its 1924 peak of 140 units, and in 1927 Möller took up taxicab manufacture after building one more nine-passenger limousine for a tour of Denmark. Some 470 Dagmars were made in all.

2 OAKLAND 6-54, 1924, USA

Though Oakland were absorbed by General Motors as early as 1909, the cars had never made the headlines, in spite of a $1,595 (£325) vee-eight launched in 1916. Oakland's sales were however to double over the next twelvemonth, thanks to their 'Sensible Six' a modest 3-litre affair using a splash-lubricated o.h.v. monobloc engine, made, like the eight, by Northway. Its 6-volt coil ignition, full electrics, cone clutch, centrally-controlled three-speed gearbox, and expanding-and-contracting brakes on the rear wheels were in no wise unorthodox, the only uncommon feature being the use of three-quarter-elliptic springs at the rear. A compact affair on a 110-inch wheelbase, it sold for $795 (£160) or $190 less than was asked for Buick's Light Six. Aluminium pistons and semi-elliptic suspension followed in 1918, by which time it was the staple Oakland. A year later the breed had edged into sixth place in home-market sales, with deliveries of 52,124 units. O.h.v. persisted until 1923, when a tourer could be bought in England for £395.

The 6-54, however, marked a step forward. It was one of the cheapest American cars with four-wheel brakes (of rod-operated, external-contracting type) as standard. It also came with detachable disc wheels, and was lighter than its predecessor, a chassis turning the scales at only 1,650 pounds. If the side-by-side valves might sound a retrograde step, pressure lubrication was adopted, and during the year Oakland pioneered the 'indestructible Duco finish' (cellulose), a quicker, cheaper process than the old ritual of paint and varnish. The price of a standard touring car was $995.

The Oakland was, however, on its way out. Like several other makers (Durant, Hudson, Buick), the Division sought a wider market with a cheap companion make, the Pontiac, announced for 1926. This sold at around $800, while Oakland prices rose to $1,095. The sales picture of 1927 told its own story; over 150,000 of the new Pontiacs as against 53,992 Oaklands, this in spite of a new 3½-litre 'All American Six'. By 1929 deliveries were down to the 30,000 mark, and an attempt to achieve a new *cachet* with another inexpensive vee-eight was a failure. No Oaklands were marketed after 1931.

3 BEAN 14, 1924, 1925,
   Great Britain

A. Harper, Sons and Bean were old-established ironfounders who sought to enter the motor industry in 1919. Much was on their side, including four ready-made munitions factories in the Dudley area, and ownership of the drawings of the successful 11·9 h.p. Perry light car. They were also members of the Harper Bean consortium, a would-be British General Motors embracing also A.B.C., Swift and Vulcan, not to mention their own sales company, the British Motor Trading Corporation, and sizable holdings in the steel business. Despite the prevailing industrial unrest, a moving assembly line was set up, and 11·9 h.p. Beans were being made at the rate of 90–100 a week when the group went bankrupt at the end of 1920.

Bean themselves survived. Under A. C. Burden's direction engine design was revised, with detachable heads and Ricardo-type combustion chambers. The 2·4-litre 14, introduced at the 1923 London Show, was a massive affair on a 114-inch wheelbase, intended also for light commercial use. The four-cylinder side-valve engine featured a positive chain drive for magneto, dynamo and fan, pistons were of alloy, and output was 32 b.h.p. Four-wheel brakes and dual ignition were catalogued options, and the car would do 55 m.p.h., though steering was very heavy. Inevitably the tourer, at £395 ($1,975) was undercut both by Morris (£320) and Austin's Twelve (£375), while production did not approach 1920 levels; at best, the weekly output of 14s was never more than forty.

Australian sales were, however, good; 731 units were sold in two seasons thanks to the exploits of Francis Birtles, culminating in an overland drive from England in 1927. The 16,000 miles took him nine months. Four-wheel brakes were standard in 1925, when the Duke of Gloucester acquired a coupé. To meet Morris competition, Bean offered a short-chassis model at £295 in 1927; this was simply a 14 engine mounted in a 12 h.p. chassis. Other contemporary changes were dural connecting-rods, and worm and nut steering in place of the earlier worm and wheel. Unfortunately at this juncture the company brought out a new Hadfield model with vee radiator and a notoriously unreliable worm-drive back end, and after 1929 they elected to concentrate on commercial vehicles until the end two years later.

4 JOWETT LONG FOUR, 1924, Great Britain

The flat-twin Jowett had a remarkable run from 1911 until 1953. Benjamin and William Jowett had already made motorcycles for Alfred Angas Scott, as well as proprietary engines, when they produced their first complete car. This was a true primitive with side tiller steering, fixed cycle-type wire wheels, and armoured wood frame. The starting handle doubled as crankcase breather, but the rest of the car was surprisingly modern; an 816 cc pressure-lubricated side-valve flat-twin engine mounted in unit with a cone clutch and a centrally-controlled three-speed gearbox; final drive was by worm. By the outbreak of war Jowetts were wheel-steered and steel-framed, and boasted not only bevel drive but also detachable steel wheels. Wheelbase was a compact 84 inches, and a two-seater weighing 860 pounds offered 43 m.p.h. for £160 ($900).

Early post-Armistice Jowetts were still two-seaters, though they had acquired Lucas Magdyno electric lighting. In 1921 engines were bored out to give a capacity of 907 cc, and coil ignition came in 1923. The cars were incredibly tough, even penetrating the narrow and slippery Bradford–Esholt sewer; a reputation confined to the make's native Yorkshire was extended when the firm exhibited at 1921's London and Glasgow shows, and two years later Jowett enthusiasts founded Britain's first one-make club. Production climbed steadily, from 10–12 a week in 1922 to 85 by 1929. Certain barbarities remained; rear-wheel and transmission brakes only were offered up to 1928, the latter being lined with asbestos string. Starters were an optional extra in 1923, but not standardized until 1926, and even on 1929 Jowetts cylinder heads were fixed, forcing mechanics to rotate the unit in the frame when decarbonizing.

The Long Four of 1923 was a successful attempt to market a full four-seater in the 7 h.p. taxation class, something never achieved by Austin, whose 'Seven' was technically an Eight. Wheelbase was 102 inches, but track remained at a narrow 45 in. The Jowett was, however, light and it could potter along at an easy 35–40 m.p.h., even if the steady beat of the flat-twin engine was not to everyone's liking. The model continued with minimal change until 1929, when some attempt was at last made to 'style' Jowetts. There were new radiator treatments in 1930, 1931, 1932 and 1934. The last of the pre-war twins retained mechanical brakes, and synchromesh did not make its appearance until 1940.

5 ROLLS-ROYCE TWENTY,
1924, 1926, Great Britain

Even Rolls-Royce were not immune from the slump of 1920–21, which persuaded them to abandon the one-model policy adopted in 1907. Characteristically, Royce chose a smaller car rather than a compromise with quality, though howls of rage attended his Twenty when it was unveiled in 1922.

There were, admittedly, several heresies. The superb four-speed gearbox with its right-hand gate change had given way to a three-speed unit affair with central lever, the handbrake was likewise centrally-located, the traditional governor had been supplanted by an automatic advance-and-retard with manual override, and single ignition (by battery and coil) sufficed. Unkind comparisons were drawn with the Buick.

Royce, however, considered three speeds sufficient. Experiments with twin o.h.c. engines had revealed but a poor return from the added complexity. He did nevertheless opt for pushrod-operated o.h.v. in a detachable head, and much of the Twenty's subsequent reputation for gutlessness was due to the immense weight of some of the formal bodies it was asked to carry. On 53 b.h.p. a tourer would cruise at 50 m.p.h., did almost all its work on top gear, and returned a frugal 22 m.p.g.

In other respects the car epitomized the best engineering practice of the period, with a seven-bearing balanced crankshaft, a Rolls-Royce-made carburetter fed by Autovac, pump and fan cooling, a single dry-plate clutch, an open propeller shaft, and a spiral bevel rear axle. The brakes, of internal-expanding type, worked on the rear wheels; the excellent mechanical-servo f.w.b. did not make their appearance until 1925. By this time, of course, the car had been brought into line with the 40–50 h.p. A standby magneto was added in 1924, and a year later four speeds with right-hand change had come to stay. Other improvements were to include hydraulic instead of friction dampers (1928), and, finally, the adoption of vertical radiator shutters in place of the archaic horizontal arrangement.

The Twenty justified its makers' hopes. A chassis price of £1,100 ($5,500) meant that a complete car with simple coachwork could be bought for £1,600, and 2,940 were delivered before the growing weight

of specialist coachwork forced Royce to enlarge the engine to 3·7 litres on his 20–25 of 1929.

6 FARMAN A6B 40CV, 1924, France

Like Hispano-Suiza and Gnôme-Rhône, the Farman brothers sought to apply aircraft-engineering techniques to luxury cars, but despite a run of twelve years their product remained very much the bridesmaid by contrast with the bride—Marc Birkigt's immortal 32CV Hispano. True, customers included the Shah of Persia, film star Pearl White, and aviator Charles Nungesser, but there were only about 120 others.

As unveiled at the 1919 Paris Salon, the car's 6·6-litre six-cylinder engine had much in common with the Hispano's; dimensions of 100 × 140 mm, vertical shaft drive for the overhead camshaft, pump and fan cooling, and vacuum feed. In some respects Waseige of Farman had the edge on Birkigt, for he opted for four forward speeds from the start, and his cooling system incorporated an ingenious, driver-controlled clutched fan. Both cars had dual ignition, the Farman favouring a magneto and coil as against the Hispano's twin coils. Initially engine and gearbox were separate, with a sub-frame to give structural strength; unit construction was adopted in 1921. In the manner of the period, the dashboard was lavishly equipped, instruments including a barometer and a gradient meter. Output was just over 100 b.h.p. at 2,800 r.p.m., but Waseige's ideas on braking were conservative, with an Edwardian rear-wheel and transmission layout.

By the time production models appeared, in 1921, a dry multiplate clutch had replaced the original cone. A chassis cost 89,000 francs, or ten times the price of a 5CV Citroën, and nearly 30,000 francs more than Panhard's new straight-eight. Servo-assisted four-wheel brakes came with the third (A6B) series in 1922.

The Farman was no mean performer: a standard tourer weighing 5,316 pounds was tested to do 90 m.p.h., while the twin-carburetter models with alloy engines, and oval-section aerodynamic coupé bodies incorporating gull-wing doors, were quite a lot faster, thanks to an output in the region of 200 b.h.p. The Farman's cantilever rear springing gave an excellent ride— 'A motor car rolls', trumpeted the company's advertising, 'A Farman glides'.

Unfortunately the alloy blocks (standardized on 1926 and later cars) proved to be porous, and big-end trouble was not unknown. Rising prices told their own story. An A6B sedan could be bought for 175,000 francs in 1925, but five years later a chassis alone retailed at 155,000, by which time the A6B had given way to the NF with duplicated steering of fearsome complexity, and a radiator of shamelessly Hispano shape; less distinctive than the original rounded

vee with its winged badge. After 1931 the Farman brothers made only aircraft.

7 MATHIS PS 10CV, 1924, France

Like his former associate Ettore Bugatti, Emile Mathis of Strasbourg became a French rather than a German manufacturer in 1918, and launched an onslaught on his new country's popular-car market, with a series of simple side-valve fours noted for high rates of rotation (his 1922 6CV was allegedly good for 4,000 r.p.m., if not for too long), four-speed gearboxes, splash lubrication, and (in some cases) differential-less back ends.

By 1920 he was experimenting with pint-sized sixes, several years ahead of the British industry. His prototype had a 1,080 cc engine and three forward speeds, but as unleashed on the public in 1922 as the PS-type, it had four speeds and 1,140 cc. Ratios were suitably rustic—6:1, 8:1, 11:5 and 20:1. The fixed cylinder head, trough-and-dipper lubrication, plate clutch, central ball change and back axle without a differential derived from his small fours. There were brakes on the rear wheels only, though front-wheel brakes and a conventional back end featured on the sporting L-type, an o.h.v. device said to be good for 70 m.p.h. Both types wore disc wheels: from 1923 onwards the PS was made with a Germanic vee-radiator. The result was a truly compact six on a

95-inch wheelbase, weighing only 1,232 pounds. Top-gear range was quoted as 3–55 m.p.h., though the latter velocity was almost certainly asking too much for the four-bearing crankshaft, while the anchors, with pedal and lever working on separate rear wheels, rendered crash stops very hazardous. By 1924 four-wheel brakes had been adopted, and a long-chassis variant, the 114-inch PSE, enabled roomier bodies to be fitted. By now the range included a boat-decked two-seater, a tourer, a cabriolet, a three-door sedan, and a full four-door sedan. Prices started at 21,000 francs, or £295 ($1,475) in England. A year later a PS tourer cost 24,000 francs; the fact that Renault's stolid 6CV could be bought for 17,450 did not matter, but now Mathis was undercut by the 10CVs of Citroën (22,230) and Peugeot (23,400), and both cars were more reliable.

1927 was to mark Mathis's zenith, with an output of 75 cars a day, but by this time he had opted for new ideas in the shape of the conventional 8CV MY, which had only four cylinders, and delivered its 25 brake horses at a more reasonable 2,800 r.p.m.

8 N.A.G. D4, 1924, Germany

In the early twenties German design was ossified by economic chaos and a depressed home market. Barred from the territories of her former enemies, the country's manufacturers concen-trated their efforts on Scandinavia and Eastern Europe, where strong suspensions counted more than sophisticated techniques. The industry took refuge in consortia; N.A.G. joined forces with Brennabor, Hansa and Hansa-Lloyd in the G.D.A. group, but this did not lead to any helpful rationalization.

The company's staple in those dark years—and one that actually earned them a profit in 1921—was the C4, a straightforward 2·6-litre side-valve four with non-detachable cylinder head, leather cone clutch, and separate, four-speed gearbox. Rear-wheel brakes and wood wheels were still standard equipment as late as 1926, and on 33 b.h.p. it was no great performer, even if its rounded-vee radiator suggested the French Delaunay-Belleville, a contemporary already headed into a long, slow decline.

Interestingly, this ponderous machine evolved into the C4b, a sports car which could and did win races albeit its proudly-proclaimed record of 78 firsts and seconds will probably not stand too close a scrutiny. A win in the 1924 *Gran Premio della Notte* at Monza (in which N.A.G. designer Riecken and his co-driver Berthold averaged 69 m.p.h. for 24 hours) was the *marque*'s best showing, but good results in the All-Russian Reliability Trials meant useful business with the U.S.S.R., and Riecken's second place (behind Caracciola's Mercedes) in the 1926 German Grand Prix was little short of sensational, bearing in mind not only the appalling weather conditions, but also Caracciola's mastery of wet roads. One suspects that the C4b's advertised 45 b.h.p. represented a very conservative estimate of its potential.

For all its detachable head and overhead valves, the 3,584-pound D4 scarcely represented serious progress; output rose only to 40 b.h.p., and no more than 55 m.p.h. were claimed. True, it was the first medium-priced German car to have front-wheel brakes as standard, but in other respects it differed little from its contemporaries. Nor was it the cheapest; at 15,000 marks (£750 on paper) it undercut the Benz at 16,500, but cost more than a Horch (14,350) or a Komnick (12,500). In the end, N.A.G.'s only safe course was the one they took; to go empire-building with the purchase of Protos and Dux (plus some new ideas), and to persevere with the heavy goods vehicles they made so well. This policy kept the wheels turning at Berlin-Oberschöneweide until 1934.

9 LOCOMOBILE JUNIOR EIGHT, 1925, USA

Straight-eights were all too often the refuge of the destitute, and the Locomobile was no exception. The company had known two golden ages, first as a volume-producer of ingenious if fragile steam runabouts at the turn of the century, and then with splendid luxury petrol cars. Their monstrous 9-litre T-head 48 was still being made at the rate of 500 a year in 1924, and would continue to be listed up to the end in 1929.

Under William C. Durant's control (he had bought Locomobile in 1922) these prestige models were left severely alone. There was, however, little future in superb coelocanths retailing at around the $9,000 (£1,800) mark, while a somewhat scaled-down L-head development, the 38, made no impression, either; so Durant went after middle-class sales with a machine that looked uncommonly like its great contemporary, the Chrysler 70. Durant, however, preferred o.h.v. to s.v., and used eight cylinders in line instead of Chrysler's six. His new power unit had a five-bearing crankshaft with Lanchester vibration damper, and was allegedly inspired by Harry Miller's racing designs. Unusual was the use of two separate heads on a monobloc engine, while the three-speed gearbox was separately-mounted. In other respects the Locomobile deviated not at all from the American norm: pump-and-splash lubrication, vacuum feed, a dry-plate clutch, and semi-elliptic springs. All brakes were of internal-expanding type. The extra pair of cylinders gave the Locomobile a longer wheelbase (124 as against 112½ inches) than the Chrysler.

Unfortunately the middle-class sector of the US market is notoriously capricious, and the Locomobile at $1,785 (£330) for a touring car was by no means the best value available. Such established Big Sixes as Hudson and

Buick (not to mention the Chrysler) were less expensive. So was Auburn's recently-introduced Eight. In 1926, Locomobile's best year, the company registered 2,064 new cars in the USA; Chrysler accounted for 129,412, which explains why the market value of a four-year-old Junior Eight was $275 (£55) by 1929. After a generation of catering for the native carriage trade, Locomobile had little chance of cashing in on export sales. The name meant nothing to Britons apart from some rather tarnished memories of a temperamental steamer.

Locomobile persevered with their own engines and minor styling changes until 1928, but the last of their 'cheap' models, though it looked like a scaled-down 48, was a bigger, Lycoming-powered eight. It also retailed at a high $2,650.

10 BEVERLEY-BARNES
24-80 H.P., 1925, Great Britain

For tax reasons straight-eights never did well in Britain; thus it is remarkable to encounter the Beverley-Barnes (the name commemorated both its native London suburb and the stream which bisected it), a *marque* which appeared annually at London shows from 1923 to 1930, always in straight-eight guise and always with an upstairs camshaft; there were two, indeed, in 1928, and thereafter.

Unfortunately, the cars were never more than a potential second line of defence for MM. Lenaerts and Dolphens, precision engineers of Belgian birth whose customers included Bentley and Invicta. Hence total production amounted to perhaps fourteen units. The original 24–80 was a big luxury machine on a 150-inch wheelbase. Its 4-litre nine-bearing engine developed 90 b.h.p., and was beautifully finished, with pressure lubrication, magneto ignition, twin Zenith carburetters, and vacuum feed. The clutch was a multiplate, and three forward speeds sufficed; a tyre pump was driven off the gearbox. Semi-elliptic springs were used in conjunction with friction dampers, and even in 1923 four-wheel internal-expanding brakes were standard, a reduction gear being incorporated in the pedal mechanism. Heavy sedans were good for 70 m.p.h., and complete Beverleys sold at around £1,100 ($5,500). Both hood and radiator were blatant cribs of the Rolls-Royce, even down to entwined 'B's on the badge. Of the five cars built, only one carried open bodywork; the last 24–80 was laid down as an ambulance chassis, but ended its days carting sheet glass around the southern environs of London.

By 1927 the 24-80 had given way to the 30-90, a more powerful 4·8-litre machine with Dewandre vacuum-servo brakes, of which only three were made. Last of the single-cam. Cars were a brace of 2½-litres with coil ignition and four forward speeds, built up on Bean chassis frames; they suffered from chronic oil starvation. From 1928 onwards the company tried a 3-litre (originally 2,736 cc) twin-camshaft design, theoretically available with a supercharger. It had an American Warner four-speed gearbox, and the radiator was 'squashed Bentley'; appropriately a winged-B badge was adopted. The death of M. Dolphens brought development to a halt after three cars had been built. Beverley's last ventures were the assembly of 4½-litre Invictas under contract, and the manufacture of a small series of twin-cam. engines for installation in the Burney Streamline cars.

11 SIMA-VIOLET, 1925, France

Few four-wheeled devices ever conformed with France's legal definition of a cyclecar, which specified a maximum weight of 350 kilograms. One that did was the Sima-Violet, of which some five thousand examples were produced between 1924 and 1928 by the Alcyon and Armor motorcycle firms as well as by S.I.M.A. themselves. It came from the drawing-board of the prolific Marcel Violet, who had been designing cyclecars since 1908, and was still at it in 1960, with plans for a racing formula based on home-made three-wheelers. Already in 1925 he had seven different makes to his credit.

The true prototype of the Sima-Violet was the S.I.C.A.M. of 1919. Its 500 cc air-cooled two-stroke flat-twin engine lived at the front of a crude frame, and the two-speed chain trans-

mission followed G.N. lines. The car sold for the equivalent of £165 ($825). By contrast, the Sima-Violet ran to a two-speed, differential-less transaxle; the flywheel magneto of early models was soon replaced by a big, high-tension affair which appeared to sit astride the single transverse front spring. Longitudinal quarter-elliptics were used at the rear, lubrication was by petroil, and the chassis was a simple tubular backbone, with angle-iron brackets to carry the plywood body, usually of open, tandem-seated type, though some rather intimate side-by-side versions were also produced. Retardation was limited to seven-inch drums on each rear wheel, operated respectively by pedal and lever. Two forward speeds (ratios were 6:1 and 16:1!) and a reverse were provided, with a separate lever (which one pushed forwards) for the latter. Lighting was of course by acetylene; there was no starter. The makers claimed 50 m.p.h., 50 m.p.g., and a tyre life of 25,000 miles, all for around £60. Other components were more fragile, though, and the manual contained stern warnings against brutal treatment.

Despite some good performances in events such as the *Bol d'Or*, and some competition work with a 750 cc flat-four development which was never marketed, the restless Violet had moved on again in 1927 to Deguingand, for whom he designed a more civilized four-cylinder two-stroke. As for S.I.M.A., they turned in 1928 to the orthodox Sima-Standard, a modernized 5CV

Citroën built up from an assortment of surplus Citroën and Amilcar bits.

12 HANOMAG 'KOMMISSBROT' 2/10PS, 1925, Germany

The Hanomag was almost a music-hall joke in Germany. It was named after the standard army loaf, and a wicked jingle going the rounds described the vehicle's ingredients as 'a bit of tin, a stroke of lacquer'. In fact, it anticipated the ideas propagandized by that outspoken journalist Josef Ganz from 1928 onwards. Ganz's credo embraced a people's car with rear-mounted, air-cooled engine, all-independent springing, and backbone frame.

The *Kommissbrot*'s vertical single-cylinder engine was water-cooled (by thermosyphon), and the frame was of orthodox type, but in other respects Ganz would have approved. Understandably, there were brakes on the rear wheels only, and the car cranked from the side, but the 500 cc power unit (which ran to pushrod o.h.v., an alloy piston, and a roller-bearing crankshaft) developed a respectable 10 b.h.p., sufficient to propel the car at 40 m.p.h. There were three forward speeds; the clutch was a single-plate, and drive was transmitted by a chain running in an oil bath to a differential-less rear axle.

The bodies were frankly unprepossessing, being aerodynamic below the waistline and (in the case of coupés) angular above it. They were strictly two-seaters, which made for plenty of legroom, while the slab sides made the most of a 41-inch track. A single, cyclops-eye headlamp in the nose was supplemented by a pair of parking lamps set high up on the cowl; electric starting was provided. A weight of 816 pounds would have put it outside the French cycle-car category, but the Hanomag sold quite well, accounting for 15,800 units between 1924 and 1928. Some were even used as single-seater taxis.

What killed it in the end was a more classic 'baby', Dixi's version of the British Austin Seven (34); the Hanomag must, however, rate as one of the Volkswagen's more serious ancestors. After 1928, its makers switched to conventional front-engined machinery, the 800 cc 3/16PS and the later 1,100 cc Garant series spanning the remaining years of peace. They were never best-sellers, though they carried on the *Kommissbrot*'s reputation for durability and were widely exported. An attempt at a comeback in 1952 with the 697 cc three-cylinder Partner came to nothing and since then the company, now associated with Henschel and Daimler-Benz, has concentrated on goods vehicles.

13 MAYBACH W3, 1925, W5, 1927, Germany

Not all German's early postwar cars were warmed-over 1912 designs; the Maybach aero-engine factory at Friedrichshafen broke new ground with their

W3, introduced in 1921. Externally the 5·7-litre six-cylinder engine (already used in Dutch Spykers) looked a trifle archaic with its side-by-side valves, fixed head, and priming cocks. It delivered its 72 brake horses at a sedate 2,200 r.p.m.; but more advanced were the dual ignition system with twelve sparking plugs, the pump cooling with driver-controlled clutched fan, and an ingenious 'flame-proof' carburetter of Maybach's own design, awkwardly mounted below the centre-line of the block.

The chassis was equally impressive, being a solid box-section affair with a wheelbase of 147 inches. The semi-elliptic springs were gaitered and assisted by friction-type dampers, and the four-wheel brakes (Germany's first) operated in alloy drums of generous dimensions. More important still, Maybach had the answer to gear-changing problems in his simple, pedal-controlled two-speed transmission of Model-T Ford type, even if the presence of a pedal-operated starter was a snare and a delusion to the careless. Everything was beautifully finished—and immensely heavy, a chassis weighing 3,655 pounds. Prices were also formidable; a chassis cost 24,000 marks, which meant something in the region of £2,200 ($11,000) for a complete car. Maybach, of course, made no bodies; these came from Auer, Erdmann und Rossi, or Killstein, and their angular styling sorted ill with the handsome, Farman-like rounded-vee radiator.

Curiously, Maybach went against accepted practice, in that he combined increasing power with more complex methods of transmitting it. The W5 of 1926 differed only from the W3 in its ultra-long-stroke 6·9-litre engine with horizontal valves operated via long rockers extending from the level of the combustion chambers to a crankcase-located camshaft. The cylinder head was detachable, and the gear-change pedal was power-assisted. Running-boards and wheel arches now formed an integral part of the frame. Yet with 120 b.h.p. available, the company's next step was the W5SG of 1928, with a two-speed, lever-controlled over-drive behind the main gearbox, which reduced revs at cruising speed from 2,400 to 1,800. Four years later came the legendary *doppelschnellgang*, which gave Maybach owners the choice of twelve ratios—eight forward plus four reverse! This featured in the last of the old-school sixes, the W6, which used the W5 engine in the vast twelve-cylinder Zeppelin frame. The inevitable results were a poor power-to-weight ratio, and poorer sales, though the W6 was still catalogued in 1934. Some seven hundred of these three series were made, 400 of them the original W3s.

14 BIANCHI S4, 1925, Italy

After 1919, Fiat enjoyed a virtual monopoly of the meagre Italian popular-car market. Most of their rivals turned to more sporting machinery,

O.M., for instance, backing their staid 469 with some faster sixes. Bianchi, however, had a healthy motorcycle business, and elected to continue their line of well-built touring models. These were seldom seen in sporting events, though the Italian Police fielded a team of S5s in the 1931 *Mille Miglia*.

Antonio Santoni's S4 was typically Italian, not only in the low and wide ratios of its four-speed gearbox, but in its looks; a simple *torpedo* body without frills, a radiator and hood which aped the Rolls-Royce, and steel artillery wheels. True, the neat three-bearing 1,287 cc pushrod engine was of a type that Fiat would not use in a touring car until 1935, but Bianchi's choice of so modest a capacity led to an output of only 26 b.h.p. Rod-and-cable operated four-wheel brakes were standard from the start, and in 1926 the car was actually cheaper (at 35,000 litre) than the 1,460cc *Tipo* 503 Fiat which it resembled so closely from the outside.

The real fly in the ointment was not, however, the 503, but Fiat's 990 cc o.h.c. 509, a true baby which began to appear in numbers (at a bargain 18,000 lire) in the latter half of 1925. The new Fiat might be undergeared and rev-happy, but it had first-class brakes, and by 1926 there was a sports version, the 509s.

Bianchi persevered with their theme. The improved S5 had acquired coil ignition by 1930, and a 30 b.h.p., 1,452 cc engine by 1932. 1934 saw the hand-some little S9 sedan with built-out boot; this one had five main bearings,

mechanical pump feed, and 16-inch wire wheels. It resembled a baby 6C 2300 *turismo* Alfa-Romeo, but two years later it had been restyled, with the beetling hood of the latest Fiats. Bonuses were hydraulic brakes and centre-lock wire wheels, but there was no synchromesh, the car was heavy, at 2,800 pounds, and 65 m.p.h. repre-sented the effective limit. Long-chassis versions, however, did well as taxis. By 1939 annual sales were down to less than 400. Not that they had ever been brilliant; fewer than 7,000 S5s had been made between 1928 and 1933. No wonder Bianchi elected to con-centrate once more on trucks and motorcycles after 1945.

15 OVERLAND WHIPPET FOUR, 1926, USA

While America remained the world's general provider, 'compacts' were no news: they were safe export business.

In 1926 Willys-Overland of Toledo were still riding high, a long way away from the receivership of 1933. Produc-tion was to reach its peak with 315,000 units in 1928, and of these nearly 240,000 were Whippets with four- or six-cylinder engines. Even in 1929, when sales dropped to below a quarter-million, the Whippet still accounted for 190,000.

Only nomenclature was complex. As introduced in June 1926 (as a 1927 (model), the car was an *Overland* Whippet, though only the first 30,000 carried the Overland script on hub caps and headlamp lenses. The 1929 and later models are sometimes called *Willys* Whippets, but either way the vehicle followed the accepted formula of a side-valve four-cylinder engine, single dry-plate clutch, three-speed gearbox, spiral bevel back axle, and semi-elliptic springing. The full-pressure lubrication was still advanced on a cheap car in 1926, as were the four-wheel brakes of the usual contracting type; not only Ford, but Chevrolet, Dodge and Star considered such refinement superfluous. Further, the car really was compact; cylinder capacity was a modest 2·2 litres, wheelbase 100 inches (the same as Model-T and three inches shorter than a Chevrolet), and overall length under twelve feet. Body styles available were roadster, touring, coach, coupé, landau and sedan, the same variety being available in the 2·7-litre Whippet Six line. An interesting feature was 'finger-tip control' on the steering-wheel, for starter, lights and horn. Early Whippets had front-opening doors, soon discarded. In Britain the cars were assembled in the Willys-Overland-Crossley plant at Stockport.

By 1929, wheelbase was up to 103½ inches, and front brakes were of expanding type. The cars remained competitive, their price range ($455–610) being rivalled only by Ford's Model-A. The Whippet Six, now with seven-bearing engine, undercut the entire six-cylinder opposition with the exception of the Chevrolet, a de luxe model retailing at $760, though Britons paid £295.

Less than 30,000 Whippets were sold in 1930, and though a 1931 edition of the Whippet Four was announced, with such improvements as double-acting hydraulic dampers and rubber engine mountings, it enjoyed only a five-month run, during which a mere 5,247 cars were made.

16 CLYNO 10·8 H.P., 1926, 1927, Great Britain

The Clyno is all too often cited as the archetype of the unsuccessful assembled car. In fact the company made a great deal of their vehicles themselves; some bodies were bought out, however, and their best model, the 10·8 h.p., used the well-tried 1,368 cc four-cylinder Coventry-Climax engine, mainstay of many a small British factory.

Clyno's main concern up to 1922 was, of course, motorcycles, but the 10·8, the work of A. G. Booth and George Stanley, was not their first car; as early as 1918, a prototype o.h.v. 10 h.p. had been built to the designs of Charles van Eugen, but then shelved. What was offered at the 1922 Show was heterodox in one respect only; it dispensed with a differential. Otherwise the ingredients were copybook; a straight-forward s.v. engine developing an average 20 b.h.p. at 2,950 r.p.m., magneto ignition, gravity feed, a three-speed gearbox, a cone clutch, and all brakes on the rear wheels. Quarter-elliptic springing was deemed sufficient and the list price of a two-seater was £265 ($1,325), or £280 with electric starting. Praiseworthy features were light steering, above-average finish and quick-detachable floorboards for easy maintenance, though speedometers were extra.

Starters, differentials and a longer wheelbase of 105 inches came in 1924, along with the option of right-hand change, standardized in 1925. 1926 cars had rod-operated four-wheel brakes, and on *de luxe* Clynos front springs were now semi-elliptic. A greater variety of body styles became available; in 1924 there were a coupé and a Weymann sedan, a better-equipped 'Royal' range was offered along with the basic types in 1925, and there was even a short-lived sports two-seater credited with 70 m.p.h. Prices kept pace hopefully with Morris; a two-seater cost £175 in 1925, but only £160 (inclusive of front-wheel brakes, which the cheapest Morrises lacked) in 1927. That year Clyno actually managed to offer a four-door sedan for under £200: the rival Morris was £4 cheaper, but had only two doors. Sales rose dramatically, from 2,026 in 1924 to a peak of 12,349 (almost all of them 10·8s) in 1926.

Unfortunately Clyno were always short of cash, and they tempted providence in 1927 by moving to a new, larger factory, and trying to make all their own engines. 1928 saw a severance with Rootes, who as distributors had been responsible for the car's excellent impact, and at the end of the season the faithful 10·8 was dropped. By May 1929, Clyno were hopelessly broke, but not before they had produced over 36,000 cars.

17 STEYR TYPE XII, 1926, Austria

The bad roads of Central Europe bred some sophisticated automobiles, if only because conditions called for excellent suspension systems. Austria, especially, was heavily dependent on exports, which explains how Steyr (whose cars were by no means utilitarian) managed to turn out 4,018 units in 1928.

The Type XII, first shown in 1925, marked Steyr's abandonment of the aggressive *spitzkühler*. It was also an early, if unusually solid example of the pint-sized six. Its mechanics were advanced, with a chain-driven overhead camshaft, a built-up, three-ball-bearing crankshaft, magneto ignition (though a coil was adopted in 1928), and the usual gravity feed. In unit with the engine were a multi-disc clutch and a four-speed gearbox; the four-wheel brakes were servo-assisted and worked in drums of generous, 13-inch diameter. Though orthodox semi-elliptic springs were used at the front, the rear wheels were independently sprung, by swing axles, a system which gave an excellent ride on all but the worst surfaces, and enabled the designer to dispense with shock absorbers.

On 30 b.h.p., performance was

unspectacular, and the car was clearly geared for mountain work with an axle ratio of 5·35:1 and a bottom gear of no less than 28:1! But the workmanship was first-rate, the price moderate (£385 in Germany or £440 in England), and 11,124 Type XIIs found buyers in five seasons. In addition to the usual tourer and fabric sedan Steyr offered a closed model with detachable top in the Lancia idiom.

In 1928 the Type XII was joined by a bigger Steyr, the 2,071 cc Type XX on a 124-inch wheelbase; an output of 45 b.h.p. called for abysmal gear ratios, but this one had centralized chassis lubrication, not to mention inspection doors in the crankcase which enabled (theoretically, at any rate) the owner to inspect the motion. A year later Ferdinand Porsche came to Steyr, and while his stay was brief, he created not only the magnificent (and lamentably abortive) 5·3-litre Austria straighteight, but also the handsome Type XXX, which used a 2·1-litre eightbearing pushrod engine in the existing Type XX chassis. The new engine was to inspire the successful six-cylinder German Wanderers of the thirties.

18 ERSKINE SIX, 1927, USA

The twenties saw a fashion among American manufacturers for cheap companion makes, the object being to widen a given breed's appeal. In Studebaker's case, however, company president Albert R. Erskine had his eyes on the European market, where high petrol prices and burdensome tax formulae called for smaller engines. The Erskine was the result of his tour of Europe in the autumn of 1924, and characteristically he chose the 1926 Paris Salon for the car's début. Even more interestingly, he ordered the Erskine's new 2·4-litre four-bearing side-valve engine from Continental, instead of making it himself.

Apart from this modest unit, which developed 40 b.h.p. at 3,200 r.p.m., there was nothing unorthodox about the Erskine; the prototype's electric pump feed and curious combination of wire wheels and demountable rims gave way on production models to the accepted arrangements—a vacuum tank and wood wheels. Internal-expanding four-wheel brakes were provided, and wheelbase was 107 inches. Sedan price was $995: English customers paid £295, £40 more than for the established Essex.

But though 26,000 Erskines were destined to find buyers overseas, the home market just did not want it. 1927, 1928 and 1929 were good years for the American industry, but during the period less than 40,000 new Erskines were registered in the USA, this despite price reductions. Not a lot was done to the design: cylinder capacity was increased to 2·6 litres in 1928, and Bendix brakes were introduced halfway through that year. Like Buick's Marquette and Oldsmobile's Viking, the Erskine found no niche. The 1930 models were the last, and they were unashamedly cheap Studebakers, publicized under the Studebaker name. Nor were they compacts; their Studebaker-built 3.4-litre engines developed 70 b.h.p., wheelbase was an average 114 inches, and sedan prices started at $985. There were no Erskines in 1931, and though Studebaker tried again with a companion make, the Rockne, in 1932, this was really only a competitor for Pontiac and De Soto, though it did better than expected in view of the prevailing recession. Studebaker were not to establish a durable foothold in the low-price class until the advent of the first of the Loewy-styled Champions in 1939. These simple and reliable flatheads would become style-leaders in 1947 and 1953, and delay Studebaker's demise by the great compact boom of 1959.

19 PACKARD SUPER EIGHT, 1927, 1928, USA

Packard's pre-eminence in the international luxury-car field between 1923 and 1939 was due to several factors. The first of these was a flat refusal to compromise over standards of workmanship; even after the arrival of the medium-priced 120 in 1935 nearly half Packard's staff of 5,100 were employed on the manufacture of the expensive Senior Eights and Twelves. The second was a contempt for styling; a 1931 Packard did not differ vastly from a 1924, and up to 1940 the only major changes in appearance were 1932's vee

radiator and 1938's vee windscreen Thus only once between 1925 and 1933 did Cadillac outsell Packard in fair fight, and at peak Packard's sales of quality cars (even the companion Six of 1920–28 was not cheap) reached remarkable levels—50,054 in 1928 alone. The company did not bother with yearly models in the accepted Detroit sense, though the Third Series ran from August 1926 to July 1927, and can therefore be loosely described as 1927. In fact the major differences between these and the Fourth Series of 1928 amounted to such refinements as cylinder wall lubrication actuated by the choke, and hood doors instead of louvres. No wonder Packard's clientele included nine royal families, from Belgium to Saudi-Arabia, Chinese war lords, Josef Stalin, and four US Presidents (Harding, Coolidge, Hoover, and Roosevelt). There was no radiator badge; the hub caps furnished the necessary identification.

The nine-bearing straight-eight had replaced the original twelve-cylinder Twin Six during 1923. As originally produced it ran to 5·9 litres and 84 b.h.p., and on a 4:1 axle ratio it was good for 80 m.p.h. Better still, the cars were well-proportioned (with wheelbases of generous length short-chassis cars measured 134 inches between wheel centres), and features included four-wheel mechanical brakes (of all-expanding type from the Second Series of February 1925), balloon tyres which eliminated the all-too-common shimmy, and detachable disc wheels. 1924 straight-eight prices started at $3,650 (£733). Second-Series cars had Bijur automatic chassis lubrication, operated by a dash-mounted plunger; and with the Third Series came the hypoid rear axle giving a lower line—three years ahead of Rolls-Royce. At the same time capacity went up to 6·3 litres and output to over 100 b.h.p. In 1929 the Six gave way to a smaller 5·3-litre Eight, other changes being the adoption of chromium plate, and the replacement of drum-type headlamps by the more elegant bullet shape.

20 DAIMLER DOUBLE-SIX-50,
1927, 1929, Great Britain

Though Packard's original twelve-cylinder car reached the public in 1915, it was not until eleven years later that a European V-12 was marketed.

In Daimler's case the motive for such a complicated device as L. H. Pomeroy's Double-Six was charmingly summarized as 'the sub-division of explosive force', and the result was certainly formidable. A 'Royal' model Fifty on the optional 163-inch wheelbase ('standard' cars were only seven-and-a-half inches shorter) measured 222 inches from stem to stern, had 110 inches of body spaces, weighed well over two tons without bodywork, and consumed petrol at the rate of 10 m.p.g. A limousine cost £2,800 ($13,000), and the 150 b.h.p. engine was so flexible that a top-gear range of 2–82 m.p.h. was claimed.

The engine was in fact a pair of 25 h.p. sleeve-valve blocks mounted at an angle of 60 degrees. Steel sleeves were used, and each bank of cylinders was an entity in itself, with its own dual ignition (by battery and coil) as well as a Daimler four-jet carburetter and water pump. The seven-bearing crankshaft incorporated a Lanchester vibration damper, and petrol was fed by air pressure from a 24-gallon rear tank. The rest of it was classic Daimler; the ratios of the separately-mounted four-speed gearbox were selected by a central lever, final drive was by under-slung worm, and the mechanical brakes had Dewandre servo assistance. Other ageless peculiarities of the breed were the push-on lever for the transmission handbrake, the three-piece double-skinned hood, the starter button concealed beneath the floor carpet, and the slatted shield protecting the fuel tank. The plated vertical strip down the radiator, traditionally the hallmark of Double-Sixes, did not in fact make its appearance (along with aluminium pistons) until 1928.

The Double-Six attracted the usual crowned heads. The first monarch to order one was King Fuad of Egypt, in 1927, though that year some existing six-cylinder Daimlers from Britain's Royal Mews had been fitted with the new engine. One of the smaller 3,744 cc Thirties was delivered to Queen Mary in 1928, and King George V ordered five Hooper-bodied cars in 1931.

The sleeve-valve Double-Six was made until 1935, though after 1931 the biggest version was a 6½-litre 40–50 with fluid flywheel transmission. The last of Daimler's traditional V-12s (1936–38) used 6½-litre pushrod engines.

21 HOTCHKISS AM2 12CV,
1927, 1930, France

Some of France's best fast tourers of the middle twenties used medium-capacity four-cylinder o.h.v. engines; the 12CV Hotchkiss was typical of these. Its true progenitor was the Englishman Harry Ainsworth, who had returned to Saint-Denis in 1923 after the Hotchkiss engine works at Coventry came under W. R. Morris's control. Ainsworth organized the new Ornano factory for a one-model policy destined to last until 1928.

In original AM-type form the 12CV was entirely straightforward. Its 2·4-litre monobloc engine had side valves in a detachable head, magneto ignition, and thermo-syphon cooling with fan assistance. This was mounted in unit with a single dry-plate clutch and a four-speed gearbox with central change. The chassis marked a return to the traditional Hotchkiss drive, abandoned briefly as an economy measure on the superseded 4-litre AL. Four-wheel brakes and wire wheels were standard, and on 48 b.h.p. open versions could approach 70 m.p.h. The car was fairly priced, at 36,500 francs for a tourer, and despite Hotchkiss's known aversion to competitions, the model annexed several class wins in hill-climbs. Some 5,000 cars were delivered between 1923 and 1926; in this latter year the AM2 saw the adoption of o.h.v., though no extra brake horses were claimed. 1927 models had dural connecting-rods, and rod instead of cable actuation for the brakes.

Not even the advent of Bertarione's admirable seven-bearing six-cylinder AM80 at the 1928 Paris Salon could break the AM2's steady run, though the horseshoe-shaped radiators became more elegant, and cars now appeared with the six's handsome semi-panelled bodies such as the 'Riviera' sportsman's coupé. It was not until 1932 that the company introduced a new four, using a short-stroke (80 × 99·5 mm) unit in a six-cylinder chassis for their new 12CV. This one had coil ignition, and was progressively developed until the end of private-car production in 1954. Even then it was destined for a new lease of life; in trucks, this time. The last of these old-school Hotchkiss engines was not made until 1964.

Ironically Ainsworth, who had left Coventry after crossing swords with Morris, was to have his revenge. In 1925, the English magnate acquired the Léon Bollée works at Le Mans, with a view to marketing Gallicized Morrises in France. The only commercially successful Morris-Léon Bollée was, however, a four-cylinder 12CV—powered by the Hotchkiss AM2 engine!

22 SINGER JUNIOR, 1928, 1930, Great Britain

Singer were Britain's no. 3 producers of private cars in 1928. Their mainstay was the 848 cc overhead camshaft Junior; with the exception of the flat-twin Jowett (4) the only full four-seater baby car as yet offered by a British manufacturer.

Heart of the car as introduced at the 1926 London Show was the two-bearing engine, which employed pump and trough lubrication and magneto ignition. It developed 16·5 b.h.p. at 3,250 r.p.m., and lived in a simple frame with only three cross-members. Three forward speeds sufficed. The inverted cone clutch, quarter-elliptic springs, rear-wheel brakes, six-volt electrics, gravity feed, and disc wheels shod with 27 × 4 tyres reflected all the best ideas of 1923. A tourer weighing 1,288 pounds cost £148 ($740), and was capable of 45 m.p.h., while a fabric sedan was introduced during the year, and Juniors featured in several publicity stunts. In 1928 a Mr and Mrs Deeley completed a 5,671-mile marathon at the Montlhéry Autodrome, averaging 39·3 m.p.h. and 34·3 m.p.g. In 1929 another car made 100 consecutive ascents and descents of Porlock Hill.

The Junior grew more sophisticated with the years; 1928's improvements were a single-plate clutch, semi-elliptic front springs, and front-wheel brakes, as well as several new bodies, among them a true convertible sedan. 1929s had semi-elliptics and hydraulic dampers all round, and aluminium pistons replaced the cast-iron type, while by 1930 the Junior had acquired coil ignition, wire wheels, chromium plating, and a top-heavy look commensurate with a weight of 1,512 pounds. The 10–30 m.p.h. acceleration time was now 15·2 seconds as against only 11 for the original 1927 tourer. Four-speed gearboxes, rear tanks and Autovac feed came in 1931, and the 1932s, last of the line, had lower and more robust frames, not to mention full-pressure lubrication. In 1933 the famous 972 cc Nine engine, still with only two main bearings, had been standardized, though the Junior's front-end sheet metal persisted on light vans until 1934.

For all the complexities of the Singer range, the Junior's sales remained steady, reaching a high point of 8,540 units in the Depression year of 1931; they never dropped below the 6,000 level after 1927. There was even an attempt (by the dying Aga concern) to build the car under licence in Germany, and a German Junior tourer (at 3,325 marks, or less than the price of a 509A Fiat) was exhibited at the 1928 Berlin Show. It never saw series production.

23 BERLIET 11CV, 1928, France

While American companies sought to market their compacts in Europe, European makers tried their luck with American-style sixes. Its detachable wheels and dynamotor apart, the 11CV Berliet, especially in roadster or fixed-head coupé form, could easily be taken for one of Detroit's lesser breeds.

The specification was conventional; a small four-bearing side-valve engine with coil ignition, a vertical Zenith carburetter fed by vacuum, and a three-speed gearbox with central change. Orthodox four-wheel mechanical brakes graced the chassis, though a practical French touch was the incorporation of a permanent baggage platform and two spare wheels at the back of the frame. For such a modest car—the original VIH of 1927 ran to only 1,800 cc—the wheelbase was a generous 120 inches, sufficient for full six-seater bodies, and Berliet claimed that the design had been subjected to two years of high-speed testing.

The inevitable variations ensued: 2-litre engines and four forward speeds had made their appearance by 1928, when a light model on a 112-inch wheelbase was also available, not to mention a 16CV VR of 2·8 litres capacity. Largest of Berliet's sixes was the 22CV VRBC, a 4·1-litre (85 × 120 mm) model made only in 1930 and 1931. Early cars had steel artillery wheels, changed for full discs in 1931. At the same time the downswept frame gave way to a straight-line type. Some six-cylinder models could be had with a *rélai*, or two-speed back axle.

Price-wise, the Berliet was fairly competitive; in 1927 its main rivals were Donnet's small six, and such hardy old fours as the 10CV Chenard-Walcker, the Hotchkiss AM2 (21), Lorraine's similarly rated o.h.v. machine, Delage's D.I, the Hotchkiss-engined Morris-Léon Bollée, and the indestructible KZ-type Renault. The Renault was the cheapest of the lot, at 25,600 francs for a chassis, but of the others only the small Chenard (26,590 fr.) undercut the Berliet.

No six-cylinder Berliets were made after 1932, when higher petrol prices bred a generation of big fours. Berliet's own 1½-litre had grown up into a 2-litre by 1939, with Peugeot-built bodywork and an ugly, Oldsmobile-like grille. After the War, however, the company elected to concentrate on heavy goods vehicles, a line of business which they have pursued with great success ever since.

24 STOEWER S10 SUPERIOR, 1928, G15 GIGANT, 1930, Germany

The straight-eight offered the twin advantages of greater flexibility and an impressively long hood, and nowhere in Europe was the disease more prevalent than in Germany, where eight manufacturers jumped aboard the bandwagon at the end of the twenties. Apart from Horch (whose overhead-camshaft designs were strictly for the carriage trade) nobody plunged more whole-heartedly into multi-cylinderism than Stoewer, who made eights only in 1929 and 1930, and offered a formidable diversity of types. The small Superior came with a choice of 2-litre

(S8) or 2½-litre (S10) engines, while the bigger Gigant was available as the G14 (3·6 litres and 70 b.h.p.), the 4-litre G15 with 80 b.h.p., and the short-chassis G15K with the same power unit, but with higher gearing. By 1930, only the G10, G15, and G15K were still catalogued, but an injection of money from the City of Stettin in 1931 led to more new eights, the 3-litre Marschall and the vast 4·9-litre Räpräsentant, this latter available on 118- or 138-inch wheelbases.

Allegedly inspired by the American Gardner, these eights all came from the drawing-board of Fritz Fiedler, later to win fame with his single-o.h.c. Horch and the six-cylinder B.M.W. family. The Stoewers were, however, entirely orthodox, with side valves, five-bearing crankshafts, coil ignition, updraught carburetters fed by mechanical pump, and four-speed unit gearboxes with central ball change. Chassis were equally unspectacular, though Ate hydraulic brakes were standard from the start. Performance varied: the S8 was underpowered and undergeared, managing only 55 m.p.h. on a 5·55:1 top gear, but the big Gigants were handsome vehicles, especially when fitted with cabriolet or tourer coachwork, in which form they were good for 80 m.p.h.

Alas! American-type eights can only pay their way when they can be built in American quantities, and the S8 at 8,000 marks was no competition for Mercedes-Benz's equally uninspired though indestructible Stuttgart Six at

the same price, let alone for a Chrysler at 7,330. That Stoewer were feeling the cold was revealed when they opened negotiations for the licence-production of Morris-Commercial trucks, and their mainstay from 1931 onwards was to be the modest front-wheel drive V5 and its descendants. The Marschall and Räpräsentant were discontinued at the end of 1932, but some thirty unsold chassis were rebodied and deliveries of the odd car continued into 1934. The Wehrmacht obligingly took another 250 Marschalls with open *Kübelwagen* bodywork.

25 IMPERIA 6CV, 1928, 1930, Belgium

Belgian manufacturers traditionally looked to well-heeled Britons to buy their admirably engineered cars; only Imperia and F.N. made serious attempts at something less costly for the home market.

M. A. Van Roggen of Imperia was wedded to the slide-valve engine, in which the slides were recessed into the cylinder walls on opposite sides, being opened and closed by double cams without any springs. The system worked reasonably well—with the snag that a rebore was a costly process involving the re-broaching of the slide housings. In other respects (apart from an engine which rotated counter-clockwise) the 6CV was an ordinary little car; its two-bearing crankshaft and splash lubrication represented the norm at the time of its introduction in 1923, and the output of its 1,100 cc engine was a respectable 24 b.h.p. The four-speed gearbox was of unit type, with low ratios necessitated by heavy bodies, but the Imperia's anchors were somewhat singular, consisting as they did of a pedal-operated transmission brake incorporating a servo, and a handbrake working on the rear wheels. These were inclined to be fierce in operation. Four-wheel brakes, always an option, were standardized by 1926, but the drums on the front wheels were merely linked to the pedal; conventional hydraulics were provided only on the last cars (1933-4). Other improvements introduced during the model's long run were coil ignition (1928), automatic chassis lubrication (1929), and radiator shutters (1931). From 1928 onwards the 6CV was joined by a 10CV six of 1,642 cc also made in 1,800 cc touring and sporting forms.

Van Roggen had sufficient faith in his slide-valve cars to go empire-building. In 1925 he attempted to organize the assembly of 6CVs in the G.W.K. works at Maidenhead, but no 'British Imperias' were ever produced, and imports were probably less than 40 cars. His domestic operations were more substantial; by 1928 the Nagant works had been acquired and turned over to making six-cylinder engines, while bodies were manufactured both by the former Matthys et Osy coachworks and by Excelsior, another of his purchases. It was also proposed that

Voisin should build Imperias under licence in France, but their contribution amounted to five 10CVs, all with sedan bodies in the Voisin idiom.

For all these brave plans, the Imperia was not destined for mass-production. The company's best year was 1930, with deliveries of 492 6CVs and 233 sixes, but thereafter output dropped steadily—353 in 1931, 184 in 1933 and only 132 in 1934, when Imperia acquired a licence to build the German f.w.d. Adler.

26 ROOSEVELT, 1929, USA

'The World's First Straight-Eight under $1,000', trumpeted Marmon's publicity in 1929. It seemed a strange boast for a firm whose previous products had included the magnificent and largely-aluminium Model-34 of 1916, though Marmon were careful to stress that the new cheap sedan was a make in its own right.

The company had, however, been addicted to eight cylinders in line ever since Barney Roos created the Little Marmon for them in 1926-7. Under his successor, Thomas J. Little, the last of the sixes had been swept away, and results appeared to justify this policy. Sales rose dramatically from 10,489 in 1927 to 15,753 in 1928, and were to pass the 22,000 mark in 1929. The Roosevelt managed not only to undercut the native opposition (its closest rival was the Studebaker at $1,345); it was also the cheapest eight on the

British market, selling for less than the unfortunate 2·6-litre Hillman, another 1929 introduction.

Though Marmon favoured o.h.v. for their bigger models, the Roosevelt engine was of straightforward five-bearing side-valve type, with coil ignition and three forward speeds. Only the hypoid back end deviated from stock American practice, but the car was quite a respectable performer, doing 65–70 m.p.h. on 70 b.p.h. A single button on top of the steering wheel controlled the starter (when pulled), the horn (when pushed), and the lights (when turned). Wood wheels and demountable rims were standard equipment, and four body styles were available, a sedan, a coupé, a convertible, and a victoria (4–5-seater coupé).

Unfortunately, as many an American maker found to his cost, cheap straight-eights were not the answer in a Depression, and the Roosevelt survived as an independent make for precisely one season. Though the R-type of 1930 was virtually the same car, apart from radiator shutters and a thermometer on the dash, the head of Theodore Roosevelt on the badge gave way to 'Marmon-Roosevelt' script on the radiator. A year later even the 'R' had gone, and Marmon's last straight-eight was the 8-125 of 1932, a big and elegant car with synchromesh, free-wheel, and power-assisted clutch, selling at $1,395 (£280). It was scarcely adequate backing for Marmon's swansong, the magnificent and costly 8-litre V-16.

27 SWIFT 10 H.P., 1929, Great Britain

Even in 1929 small manufacturers could still make ends meet on limited runs of a simple product, and it was not prim-arily lack of sales that killed Swift two years later. Their annual production averaged around 1,800 units, and their staple was the rugged little three-bearing side-valve four-cylinder Ten, costing £220 ($1,100) with touring body. The monobloc engine, designed by W. Radford, had been around since 1919, and had roots going back a long way further.

1929's 3P series probably represented the model's zenith, in that it retained the traditional radiator, fixed, bicycle-crank-type starting handle, and nickel plating (all to disappear on the 1930 models), but had all the necessary improvements of the era. The single-plate clutch and four-wheel brakes were legacies from the QA-series of 1926, while the current 1,190 cc engine (which propelled four-seaters at 50–55 m.p.h. on a nominal 22 b.h.p.) had arrived with the first P-type of 1927. Four forward speeds were 1929's principal novelty, and the season's fabric sedan style with its optional sun-shine roof had a lot more character than the mock-American six-window edi-tion fitted to the 1930 (4P) and 1931 (5P) models, with their chromium-plated, ribbon-type radiator shells.

Engine design had remained fairly constant throughout the Ten's career. Capacity of the original 1919 version had been 1,122 cc (63 × 90 mm); this and its separate three-speed gearbox were mounted in a sub-frame in a simple chassis with semi-elliptic springs. Ignition was by magneto, the footbrake worked on the transmission, and the 12-volt electrics (with starter) were something of a luxury on a £450 car. A short 90-inch wheelbase made it strictly a two-seater, though 50 m.p.h. and 50 m.p.g. were claimed. By 1922, all brakes were on the rear wheels. The Q-type of 1923 represented an attempt at a competitive price, with a smaller 1,097 cc engine, quarter-elliptic front springs, disc wheels, 6-volt coil ignition, and a three-lamp lighting set; weight was only 1,400 pounds. Some of the refinement returned in 1925, with a reversion to magneto ignition and five lamps, as well as well-base wheels. An extra nine inches of wheelbase allowed for full four-seater bodies, and (inevitably) lower gearing. The price of an open car was £235.

The last Swift Tens came in 1931, distinguishable by the vertical chromium-plate strip down the centre of their radiators, and by their rear-mounted petrol tanks. An attempt to save the day with an 8 h.p. model at £160 proved unavailing.

28 LA LICORNE 5CV, 1929, 1930, France

Most Corre-La Licornes were small, utilitarian vehicles with proprietary engines, initially by de Dion and later by Ballot, though there had been a de Dion-powered 35CV vee-eight in 1910. The 5CV, however, used their own power unit, and sold on its 'dressy' looks at a time when its mass-produced rivals were pedestrian in style.

Mechanically the car was fairly ordinary. Cylinder dimensions of 60 × 80 mm were a little advanced for 1928, but the engine itself was a straightforward two-bearing side-valve with pressure-fed crankshaft, magneto ignition, and alloy pistons. Circulation was by thermo-syphon, the gearbox boasted three speeds, and the frame was a simple affair with three cross-members. The vehicle rode on quarter-elliptic springs, but foot and hand brakes alike worked on all four wheels, and starting was by silent dynamotor. A longish wheelbase of 96½ inches left room for four-seater bodies, La Licorne's own styles being supplemented by the work of such specialists as Duval, Kelsch, and Manessius. Especially attractive were the 1930–31 models, which embraced everything from light vans and *torpédos commerciaux* to the 'Femina' two-seater cabriolet and the 'Deauville' *coach-luxe*, or sportsman's coupé with rear trunk. Prices ran from 14,000 to 20,000 francs, which made the 5CV competitive with Rosengart's French-speaking Austin Seven, the little Mathis, and the Peugeot 201.

For all its pretty looks, the Licorne attracted favourable press notices. A top-gear range of 3–50 m.p.h., good brakes, excellent hill-climbing capabilities and a 36 m.p.g. thirst were noted, one French reporter observing that it 'felt like a much bigger car'. A latter-day owner described his 1930 sedan as '*absolument inusable*'. In the Monte Carlo Rally, H. Petit took sixth place in 1928, capping this with an overall win in 1930; the Licorne, incidentally, was the smallest car to win a 'Monte' before 1958.

In later years the 5CV grew up into an 1,130 cc 6/8CV, the L04, but small s.v. fours with two-bearing engines (now with i.f.s. and synchromesh) were still being made in 1937.

29 PRAGA ALFA, 1929, 1930, Czechoslovakia

In 1929 Czechoslovakia's well-protected motor industry was selling most of its annual output of 10,000-odd private cars on the home market, a state of affairs which made for ranges as complicated as those of Renault or Fiat. In Praga's case this meant a small car, the Piccolo, which grew up steadily from 707 cc to 995 cc; the medium-sized Alfa; and bigger sixes and straight-eights. All were designed by Ing. Frantisek Kec, who came to the factory in 1911 and remained active there until the German Occupation. Kec's thinking was orthodox; though he was to follow the prevailing Central European fashion for all-independent springing and backbone frames in the middle 1930s, he stuck firmly to side-valve

engines. Only one o.h.v. Praga private car saw the light of day, and that was the prototype Lady sports two-seater of 1938.

The Alfa of 1927 was, remarkably, a small six. Its 1,496 cc engine developed 26 b.h.p. at 3,000 r.p.m., and its 6-volt coil ignition, plate clutch, four-speed gearbox and semi-elliptic springs followed international form for the period. A 118-inch wheelbase catered for family-sized coachwork, and appearance was pedestrian. The only unusual feature was found in the brakes, for Kec, like George Lanchester, combined mechanical actuation with hydraulic servo assistance. Full hydraulics were not adopted until 1936.

Like most of the more successful sixes, the Alfa grew up with the years, and the 17th Series of 1930 ran to 1,795 cc and 38 b.h.p., as well as 12-volt electrics. Top speed went up from 55 to 65 m.p.h., and these cars would cruise all day at 50. By the mid-thirties, Praga had gone over to four cylinders in the 1,500–2,000 cc class. and their 1935 Super-Piccolo affected outlandish aerodynamic sedan bodywork with styled headlamps and spatted wheels. There was still a six-cylinder Alfa in the range, but this had a 2½-litre engine, i.f.s., and the choice of synchromesh or Cotal electric gearboxes. Praga sales remained steady rather than spectacular, fluctuating between 500 and 1,000 in the early Depression years, and reaching a peak (thanks to the elegant little Baby) in 1934, when they led the native industry with 2,250 cars delivered, as against 2,192 Tatras and only 1,629 Skodas.

30 MAGOSIX, 1929, Hungary

Industrially, Hungary suffered worst from the carve-up of the Hapsburg Empire in 1919. The Dual Monarchy's major car producers (Austro-Daimler, Gräf und Stift, Laurin-Klement, Nesselsdorf, and Praga) were divided between Austria and Czechoslovakia, while Rumania got the Marta works at Arad. Thus the new republic was left with virtually no indigenous private cars. Her main automobile contribution has always been trucks; even today this state of affair still obtains, with only commercial vehicles (Csepel, Ikarus) being made.

None of the country's inter-War *marques* were exported. The two-stroke Weiss Manfred would have remained in total obscurity but for Victor Szmick's second place in the 1929 Monte Carlo Rally, the Meray was a JAP-engined cyclecar, and Mavag's Budapest factory produced German Fords under licence. Only the cars of the Magyar Altalanos Gepygar achieved any currency, with production (on Hungary's first assembly line) running at as many as 1,500 units a year. The first 1·8-litre four cylinder machines, introduced in 1920, were known as Magomobils, their six-cylinder successors of 1927–35 as Magosixes, and taxi versions bore the

Magotax name. The Magosix was also offered as a light van or truck.

The vehicle was cast in the usual contemporary Euro-American mould, and styling was typical 1928 Fiat, with stolid, boxy bodies, rectangular radiators, and steel artillery wheels. Four forward speeds were used on the more powerful models, three sufficing on the smaller species, but all Magosixes had hydraulic brakes. Otherwise the only variations were those of capacity and output. Private cars came with 1,991 cc, 2,112 cc, and 2,443 cc side-valve units developing 40, 45, and 50 b.h.p. respectively. Like Fiat, whose 520 may well have inspired the Hungarian car, M.A.G. favoured a small-bore 59 × 100 mm (1,638 cc) engine, rated at 30 b.h.p., for their cabs. Production ceased in 1935, but many taxis were still at work until well into the 1950s.

31 VOLVO PV651, 1929, PV653, 1933, Sweden

The Swedish motor industry still amounted to little, as indeed did Swedish motoring. The majority of the 127,000 private cars registered in 1927 were of American origin, which explains why Assar Gabrielsson and Gustaf Larson, the founders of Volvo, opted for an American type of vehicle. With the aid of finance from SKF, they had their first model, the 1·9-litre four-cylinder 'Jakob', in production by 1927. Two years later it gave way to the first of a series of s.v. sixes destined to survive into 1958, the last manifestations of the theme being the PV821/831 taxi and the TP21 four-wheel-drive command car for the army. While Volvo's international reputation derives from the o.h.v. four-cylinder PV444 of 1944, the company had a modest foothold in the Low Countries by 1939, and were exporting a handful of cars alongside their established trucks.

The PV651 was an orthodox 3-litre six with three-speed gearbox, but both synchromesh and hydraulic brakes made their appearance early in the model's run. Wood artillery wheels were standard, but only one of the twin side-mounted spares was genuine; the other's leather cover concealed the tool kit. Standard versions had a 116-inch wheelbase, and weighed around 3,300 pounds, but there was also a long-chassis seven-seater (TR670) with wheelbase options of 122 or 128 inches. These were destined for taxi service; an initial batch of 200 proved inadequate, and eventually no fewer than 659 (plus 2,382 of the original PV651s) were delivered before the factory switched to the PV653–655 series, with 65 b.h.p., 3¼-litre engines, more rounded lines, free wheels, and twin reversing lamps on *de luxe* versions. A parallel seven-seater was also offered, but in 1935 these types gave way after a run of 1,800-odd units to the PV656, last of the beam-axled Volvos, which had an inclined vee-radiator.

Thereafter the stylists moved in, and

some rather unfortunate shapes ensued. The PV36 Carioca of 1935–38 was a 75 m.p.h. motor-car (65 was about the limit on earlier editions), but was a too convincing imitation of Chrysler's Airflow. A year later came a return to exposed headlamps on the PV51, a more compact vehicle on a 113¼-inch wheelbase, while the PV53 family, which saw Volvo through the War, looked like a cross between a Chevrolet and a Plymouth, and were designed to run on charcoal as well as on petrol; in the former case output dropped from 84 to 50 b.h.p. Last of the sedan series was the PV60 (1946–50), a Plymouth-styled fastback with column change, optional overdrive, and 90 b.h.p. In all, 26,152 s.v. sixes were made.

32 PIERCE-ARROW EIGHT, 1930, USA

Despite the Studebaker take-over of 1928 (the alliance lasted till 1933), Pierce-Arrow's new 1929 eight-cylinder owed nothing to Studebaker influence, even if some castings and bodies emanated from South Bend.

Though overshadowed by the later V-12 of 1932, the straight-eight (which had nine main bearings to the five of Studebaker's President) was just as well made, and also economic to produce. 8,422 were made in 1929, and a respectable 6,795 in 1930. The 5.9-litre s.v. engine developed 125 b.h.p. at 3,000 r.p.m., the block and crankcase were of cast iron, the camshaft was chain-driven, and fuel feed was by mechanical pump. A twin dry-plate clutch was used, and three forward speeds were standard, though a four-speed box with silent third was available until 1931. The massive frame (wheelbase options were 133 and 143 inches) had side-members eight inches deep, and Pierce, like Packard, used a hypoid rear axle which lowered the body line and gave the cars an elegance lacking in their immediate predecessors. Every Pierce body, incidentally, received fourteen coats of lacquer and seven complete inspections, while rear axles were tested for silence in a sound-proof room. As always, most Pierces wore their headlamps half-streamlined into the front wings, but these were not compulsory. 1929 prices ran from $2,775 to $5,750 (£555–1,250).

1930 models came in three ranges, the biggest of which used a 6·3-litre, 132 b.h.p. engine, while handbrakes now worked on the rear wheels instead of on the transmission. Four-wheel handbrakes and free wheels came in 1931, and 1932 cars had box-girder frames of wider track, bigger, servo-assisted brakes, eight-point rubber suspension for their engines, synchromesh, and Startix automatic starters. Bodies were sound-insulated.

The company might assert, in 1937, that 'until individuality ceases to be an American trait', it would 'continue to strive for distinction in the motor cars it builds', but such a policy could not pay, even when trailer homes were added, desperately, to the programme. The 1937 Eight was a magnificent carriage, with hydraulic valve lifters, no-draught ventilation, an overdrive, a defroster, and a speedometer also calibrated in R.P.M.; its 150 brake-horsepower might cope effortlessly with a weight of 5,676 pounds; but prices started at $3,195, or about double the money asked for a basic Cadillac sedan. Cadillac and La Salle sold some 45,000 cars that year: in their penultimate season, Pierce-Arrow disposed of precisely 167.

33   SALMSON S4, 1930, France

Though Salmson made their name with *cyclecar-voiturettes* and small sports models, they were marketing a twin-overhead-camshaft tourer, the D-type, as early as 1922; thus the relatively sedate S4 of 1929 came as no surprise to those who were aware of the Board's dislike of the racing programme conducted on a shoe-string by designer Emile Petit. In any case, the demand for 1,100 cc sporting types had virtually dried up; already there had been a stillborn 1·6-litre six, the S6, at the 1928 Salon, and henceforward Salmson's thinking was to centre on small luxury sedans of some performance.

Not that the S4 did not bear signs of its sporting lineage; the pressure-lubricated three-bearing twin o.h.c. 1,300 cc engine was inspired by the GS unit; other heritages were the magneto (made by Salmson themselves), the gravity feed, and thermo-syphon circulation, the rod-operated four-wheel brakes, and the centre-lock wire wheels. True, the Cross of Saint Andrew had vanished from the radiator, replaced by a new design by artist André Kow. Though not spectacularly fast at 65 m.p.h., the S4 did not really justify Petit's angry resignation, for it handled well and could outperform average 2-litre family sedans like the Berliet (23). No fewer than ten body styles were available, and the price was a modest 19,900 francs, which explains why nearly 3,500 were sold, mostly at home, during the Depression years.

Inevitably the car grew up, evolving in 1933 into the 1,471 cc S4C, with four speeds, rear tank, dual ignition, stiffer frame, duo-servo brakes, and vertical radiator shutters. If a trifle undergeared and heavy to steer at low speeds, the new Salmson would hold an easy 4,000 r.p.m.; some 250 were made under licence (with British-style bodywork) by British Salmson Aero Engines at Raynes Park. Synchromesh (always found on these latter) replaced the original crash box on the native article in May, 1934. The S4D of 1935 ran to 1·6 litres and 47 b.h.p.; it also had i.f.s., rack-and-pinion steering and a Cotal electric gearbox, though synchromesh was still an option. The twin-cam Salmsons, though no longer light cars in any sense of the word, were to survive until the company's demise in 1957; even 2·3-litre versions were

rated at a mere 13CV, which put them on the safe side of the fiscal abyss created by post-war French Governments.

34 BMW-DIXI 3/15PS, 1930, 1931, Germany

While other German makers sought to ape American ways with large sixes and eights, the old-established Dixi concern acquired a manufacturing licence for Britain's Austin Seven in 1927. Its uncoupled four-wheel brakes, 'spit-and-hope' lubrication, and bouncy suspension (by a transverse leaf spring at the front, and longitudinal quarter-elliptics at the rear) were well-proven, even if the car did not live up to the Latin implications ('It's The Last Word') of the brand-name under which it was sold in Germany.

Dixi were not, of course, the only foreign factory to take this safe route to instant baby-car manufacture. A year later Lucien Rosengart would be producing Austins in France, and the first American variants issued from Butler, Pennsylvania, in the summer of 1930.

Apart from the 6-volt Pöge coil ignition (Austins still retained their magnetos in 1927) and left-hand drive, early Dixis followed their English prototypes faithfully, and it was not until the BMW motorcycle firm took over in 1929 that such stylistic differences as a wider radiator and horizontal hood louvres made their appearance.

Either way, Austin did well out of the deal, to the tune of a 2 per cent royalty on every car. Price of a tourer was only 2,800 marks (£140), and by 1929 the 3/15PS was available in Denmark for £10 less. Production was running at 350–400 a month in 1930, when a sedan retailed at £125, and BMW were offering factory-financed hire purchase. Some 20,000 of the basic design were turned out, in addition to another 150 of the Wartburg Sport, a pointed-tail two-seater in the style of Austin's Ulster, though its lightly-tuned engine developed a mild 18 b.h.p. on a 7:1 compression. Six body styles were listed in 1931, when a few thousand Dixis were made with transverse-leaf i.f.s., a halfway house between the old Longbridge idiom and Fritz Fiedler's first true BMW. Outwardly this latter was almost pure Austin, but under the skin Teutonic progressiveness was only too apparent. The pressure-lubricated 788 cc o.h.v. engine retained its two-bearing crankshaft, but output was now a respectable 20 b.h.p.; all wheels were independently sprung, and the frame was a backbone. Unfortunately weight had soared; the old 3/15PS turned the scales at 853 pounds, but the 3/20 sedan's 1,450 pounds called for an abysmal 5·9:1 axle ratio. Though sixes were destined to engage most of BMW's energies after 1934, a little-known 845 cc four, the 309, was still offered in 1936. It shared both the chassis and body styles of the 1½-litre 315.

35 FN 1625, 1930, 1931, Belgium

FN's attitude during the long, slow decline of the Belgian automobile industry was more realistic than that of their competitors. It could afford to be, for their principal business remained small arms, with motorcycles a good second. None the less, the small o.h.v. four they introduced for 1924 had a long run, terminating nearly nine years later, and sales of 7,302 cars during this period justified their policy.

First of the series was the 1300 with 1,327 cc engine, three-speed unit gearbox, thermo-syphon cooling and (even in 1924) four-wheel brakes actuated by pedal and lever alike. It was a full four-seater on a 108-inch wheelbase, and the subsequent 1300D had four speeds, a marked improvement on the low and wide ratios of the original edition. It spoke volumes for the power unit that the car would do 40 m.p.h. in second! Interestingly, a sporting edition (the 1300 Sp) swept the board in the 1,500 cc category of the 1924 and 1926 Belgian 24-Hour Races.

Coil ignition arrived in 1928 on the 1450, a 68 × 100 mm development; on these cars the handbrake worked on the rear wheels only, and the stock body was a ponderous six-window sedan with rear trunk and wood artillery wheels, though wire wheels and a hood strap were worn on the sporting versions, said to be capable of 80 m.p.h. 1930 saw bigger, 1,628 cc engines and chromium plating, but for all their stolid looks, these later o.h.v. FNs were very tough, a works team going through the 1931 Alpine Trial without trouble. Another car took on the Brussels–Gibraltar express, and beat it by eight hours. Even more remarkable was the exploit of a party of army officers, with two 1450s, who set off from Luxembourg in May, 1928, to drive to the Cape. Three-and-a-half months later, one car arrived at its destination (the other had blown itself up in a Tanganyikan bush fire), having averaged 150 miles a day, the first production sedan to drive overland from Algiers to the southern tip of Africa.

The French trend towards bigger utility machines was followed in Belgium, where the 1625 gave way in 1933 to the 2·1-litre s.v. Baudouin, a dull and well-appointed affair, with three forward speeds and *conduite intérieure avec malle* bodywork which made it hard to distinguish from an 8CV Renault. Neither this nor its successor, the 2,260 cc Prince Albert with four-speed synchromesh gearbox and rather prettier bodies, could save FN's private-car department, which closed down during 1935.

36 CHRYSLER CD, 1931, USA

With only seven seasons of automobile manufacture behind him in 1931, Walter P. Chrysler had an impressive record. His original Chrysler 70 of 1924 had been an instant success, thanks

to its hydraulic four-wheel brakes and balloon tyres, his sporting roadsters had frightened the Bentleys at Le Mans, and by 1928 his prestige Imperial Six disposed of 112 b.h.p. as America's most powerful touring car. In the meantime he had absorbed an established maker (Dodge) and launched two new breeds (De Soto, Plymouth) to give his empire full coverage of the home market. Now he came out with a brace of straight-eights, distinguished by low-built lines and long hoods which aped the f.w.d. Cord.

Prestige model of the range was, of course, the vast 6·3-litre Custom Imperial with nine-bearing 135 b.h.p. engine, capable of 96 m.p.h. in return for a fearful thirst. Despite a wheelbase 21 inches shorter, the CD looked almost as impressive, especially in roadster form with fold-flat screen and two-tone cellulose. The engine was a simpler, five-bearing affair, but the mechanical pump feed, internal-expanding hydraulic brakes (with transmission handbrake), and thermostatically-controlled radiator shutters were similar, as was curiously, the four-speed gearbox, then in vogue in Detroit. Not that this was a novelty; even in 1918, when design was becoming stereotyped, no fewer than nine major American makes used four speeds, and Packard and Pierce-Arrow (32) also offered such transmissions in 1931. Chrysler called theirs a 'twin-top' box, and this is what it was, ratios being an odd assortment (4·1, 5·67, 10·18, and 14·7 to 1). The CD sold for $1,565 in its homeland or £577 in Britain, and speeds on the two upper ratios were 73 and 60 m.p.h. All cars were wired for radio at the factory.

Evidently the original CD was underpowered, for cylinder capacity was increased twice during the season. Cars built in the first part of the model's run had 4-litre (3 × 4¼ in.) engines; the piston stroke was left untouched, but the bore went up, first to 3⅛ in., and then to 3¼ in., boosting output from an average 80 b.h.p. to a respectable 100. Four speeds were not used after 1933; engines were now powerful enough to do their work without such aids, and in 1934 Chrysler adopted automatic overdrive, a more painless means of achieving a high cruising gear.

37 DE VAUX 6-75, 1931, USA

To seek entry to the closed shop of the US automobile industry at any time was to tempt providence (even Henry Kaiser failed after World War II); but to stage one's attempt at the depth of the Depression in 1931 was to court disaster, as the brief and stormy career of the De Vaux and its descendants reveals. Launched at Grand Rapids, Michigan, in April of that year, it died nine months and 6,038 cars later, only to reappear as the Continental Ace in 1933, under the sponsorship of the famed Continental proprietary-engine firm. There were also Canadian De Vaux and Continental cars, sold under the Frontenac name by Dominion Motors.

In fact the 6-75 was not entirely new. Its sponsors, Norman De Vaux and Colonel Elbert J. Hall, entered the motor business by buying two plants (in Grand Rapids, and Oakland, Cal.) from the dying Durant empire, and the car had a lot in common with the Durant Six, though it was better-looking. Specification was entirely conventional, with four-bearing side-valve engine, full-pressure lubrication, mechanical pump feed, a three-speed silent-second gearbox of Warner manufacture, mechanical brakes, and semi-elliptic suspension. Output was an average 65 b.h.p. from 3½ litres, and a sedan on a wheelbase of 112 inches weighed 2,785 pounds. Six basic body styles were offered, with variations in wheel equipment (fixed wood, and detachable wire with or without the then fashionable dual sidemounts), and a standard sedan at $695 (£140) was priced exactly midway between a Chevrolet at $635 and a Pontiac at $745.

Unfortunately the first five months' sales of nearly 4,000 cars proved a false start, and the 1932s with more powerful, rubber-mounted engines, free wheels, and raked windscreens hardly sold at all. Plans for overseas marketing came to little despite special export variants, distinguishable by their transmission handbrakes. As for the Continental Ace, this handsome sedan with Graham-like body should have been an attractive proposition at $745, but only

651 were made. Continental fared only a little better with their cut-price ($335, or £67) Beacon, a 2·2-litre four. By October, 1934, they were reduced to a clearance sale, with new bodies offered at $47·60 each. For 95 cents, too, the nostalgic could buy surplus examples of De Vaux's optional-extra Flying Girl mascot. Norman De Vaux was to try again in 1936 with yet another cheap and compact four, the De-Vo, but this never passed beyond the prototype stage.

38 STAR COMET EIGHTEEN,
1931, 1932, Great Britain

Wolverhampton was justly nicknamed the 'Capital City of the Lost Causes', and by 1931 the Star Motor Company was perched on the edge of limbo, though the Guy take-over of 1927 had given them a new and spacious plant in place of the old, downtown rabbit-warren of workshops. Never style-leaders, Star's products were none the less solid, upper-middle-class machines of some refinement, even if the 18-50 hardly deserved the label of Light Six attached to it when it was introduced at the 1927 London Show. The most that could be said was that it was appreciably lighter than the existing 20-60 with its 135-inch wheelbase and formal bodywork.

Mechanically it typified its category, with 2½-litre pushrod engine, detach-able head, alloy pistons, single-plate clutch, four forward speeds, and open propeller-shaft. Such accepted U-features as magneto ignition and right-hand gear-change remained, though the gearbox was now in unit with its engine. A robust chassis rode on semi-elliptic springs, and a 120-inch wheel-base lent itself to commodious bodies, though the artillery wheels did nothing for the car's looks. At £450 ($2,250) it was fairly priced, and its top speed was an average 60 m.p.h. By 1930, it had acquired some elegance, thanks to wire wheels, chromium plating, and bodies such as the 'Jason' close-coupled coupé —Star, as always, favoured astronomical nomenclature.

Outwardly, the Comet of 1931 was entirely new, with chromium-plated hubcaps, side-mounted spare wheel, two-tone finish, a new radiator with central vertical bar (another indirect Cord legacy!), and the now fashionable high waistline with shallow screen. On the mechanical side gimmickry was the order of the day, with a silent third gear, centralized chassis lubrication, and built-in jacks, while for £495 the car offered a useful 75 m.p.h. In 1932, Star tried hard, with the existing Comet, a bigger 3-litre Comet 21 on the same 123-inch wheelbase, the 3·6-litre Planet for the carriage trade, and a new 14 h.p. Little Comet with 2·1-litre seven-bearing engine, coil ignition, and central change. This was a rolling accessory shop; sliding roof, stop and reversing lamps, dual wipers, fog-lamps, permanent jacks, and folding tables, all for a modest £345. Unfortunately, the mass-producers were also becoming gimmick-minded, and that Spring Guy Motors quietly closed the Star factory down for good.

39   TRIUMPH SCORPION,
1931, 1932, Great Britain

The Scorpion was a direct crib of the Wolseley Hornet theme, even down to nomenclature, only this time the raw material was Triumph's Super Seven, and not the Morris Minor. It consisted of a Super Seven chassis lengthened just sufficiently to accommodate two extra cylinders; what it lacked was any additional bracing.

In cold print the formula added up to a tiny, four-bearing six-cylinder s.v. engine of 1,203 cc, married to a dry-plate clutch, a three-speed gearbox, and Triumph's durable worm-drive back end. A strong point was the use of hydraulic brakes with 9½-inch drums, though the price of such sophistication was a transmission handbrake of the sudden-death variety. Astonishing flexibility (4–63 m.p.h. in top) was won by the use of a 6·25:1 axle ratio, while one of the penalties of compact dimensions (the pretty Scorpion two-door coupé was only 137 inches long) was a narrow 42-inch track, giving a bumpy ride accentuated by the retention of the Super Seven's quarter-elliptic rear springs. Poor weight distribution made the steering heavy, and limited the car's appeal to lady motorists. At £237 ($1,185) it was, however, inexpensive enough, like the La Licorne (28) to attract those with modest means and a desire for something different.

An extra six inches of wheelbase and semi-elliptics at the rear were 1932's principal improvements, while the fuel tank was moved to the rear and *de luxe* models with six-window sedan bodies (now called Twelve-Sixes in the interests of a new image!) had four-speed gearboxes. Not surprisingly, the Scorpion attracted the attention of the custom coach-builders, though its limited production (about 1,250 all told) prevented it from matching the small Wolseley's popularity. In 1932, however, specialists such as Abbey, Jensen and Maddox could muster five variations on the Triumph theme, all retailing for less than £270.

It was, however, a change of direction rather than the Scorpion's inherent weaknesses that killed it. The miniature six was still in the 1933 catalogue, now with 96-inch wheelbase, four speeds, and built-in jacks, at a bargain £195, but the advent of a new management at Triumph led to a line of elegant semi-sporting machinery, suitable for family use, and these Glorias would dominate their thinking until the end of 1936.

40   DKW F1-500, 1931, Germany

The Dane Jorgen Skäfte Rasmussen had made his name with DKW (*Das Kleine Wunder*) two-stroke motor-cycles, before he turned his hand to cars in 1928. The first P-type was an ingenious utility machine powered by a water-cooled 16·5 b.h.p. vertical-twin two-stroke unit of 584 cc, mounted in unit with a three-speed gearbox. The crankshaft ran in three roller bearings, and lubrication was by petroil. Mechanical four-wheel brakes and all-round transverse suspension also featured, but cleverest of all was the structure, for there was no chassis, and the unitary body was of (allegedly) fire-proof wood construction with artificial leather covering. The makers thoughtfully lined the engine compartment with sheet metal, just to make sure! The sports two-seater version weighed only 1,092 pounds, and during 1930 one of these cars averaged 56·86 m.p.h. for twenty-four hours.

Front-wheel drive came in 1931 with the F1 (there was also a F2 using the P's bigger engine). This set the pattern not only for subsequent twin-cylinder DKWs, but also for their post-war derivatives (SAAB in Sweden, I.F.A. in East Germany, and Syrena in Poland). The 'chassis' was limited to a double backbone with outriggers to carry the body, but the engine (which incorporated a dyna-starter) was set across the frame in unit with its multiple-wet-plate clutch and three-speed box. All wheels were independently suspended by double transverse springs, and in its basic two-seater form the little DKW weighed just under 1,000 pounds. It could be bought for the equivalent of £84 ($420); top speed was around the 50 m.p.h. mark.

Sales were a little slow at first: 4,353 in 1931–2, rising to an average of 13,000 a year by 1934–5, and reaching

their zenith in 1937, when 39,593 found buyers. In 1932 Rasmussen formed his Auto Union consortium (Audi, DKW, Horch and Wanderer); henceforward DKWs wore the *vier ringe* badge and more elegant, inclined radiators in the Horch style. Standard models were the 584 cc 18 b.h.p. Reichsklasse, and the 684 cc Meisterklasse with 20 b.h.p., not to mention such refinements as a free wheel and centralized chassis lubrication. A longer, 102-inch wheelbase meant comfortable four-seat sedan and cabriolet bodies, and weight was kept down to 1,512 pounds. Acceleration was leisurely thanks to a wide-ratio gearbox, while the inverted L-action of the dashboard-mounted gear lever was a trifle awkward; the DKW would, however, cruise happily at 45 m.p.h. Fabric bodies continued to feature on Reichs- and Meisterklasse models up to 1939–40, though from 1936 onwards the company also listed two- and four-seater coachbuilt *luxus* cabriolets, which resembled miniature editions of the Type 853 Horch. They were also extremely expensive; the English price was £259, or £100 more than the utilitarian Meisterklasse.

41 MARTINI NF, 1931, 1934, Switzerland

The name of Martini no longer had any international significance by 1931; in fact, most of the 300 cars the company had delivered three years earlier had been German 2½-litre six-cylinder Wanderers built up from imported parts. These were at least a more economic proposition than the latter-day *pur sang* Martinis produced under the guidance and financial support of the Steiger brothers, already known for the sports cars they had made in Germany. Their big side-valve sixes, the 3·1-litre FU and the 4·4-litre FUS, were made until 1929-30, later ones featuring twin horizontal Zenith carburetters, four forward speeds, and Westinghouse vacuum-servo brakes; a Maybach-built overdrive was available to order. Some experiments with o.h.v. in 1929 produced nothing beyond a trading loss of 940,000 Swiss francs the following year. Even the home market no longer bought patriotically, for a census taken in 1929 showed that less than one per cent of Switzerland's 55,149 private cars were Martinis.

Thus the NF arrived in an arid climate, which it did nothing to alleviate. It was a beautifully-made machine on a 138-inch wheelbase, weighing a good two tons in sedan form; magneto ignition was retained for its 4·4-litre s.v. six-cylinder engine, which developed an adequate 95 b.h.p. at 3,000 r.p.m. The four-speed gearbox incorporated a silent second, brakes were hydraulic (with a transmission handbrake) and other features included hydraulic shock absorbers and centralized chassis lubrication. Final drive was by worm, and 1933 saw the provision of servo assistance for clutch and brakes, as well as the adoption of synchromesh. Sales were, however, down to sixty cars, though the custom-

ers included one cantonal prison, which used its NF to chase escaped convicts! The NF's excellent hill-climbing powers justified the mountain-goat emblem on the radiator, which replaced the traditional guns in Martini's declining years. The decline came to its end with the closure of the factory in 1934.

42 GRÄF UND STIFT SP8, 1931, 1933, Austria

The 'Rolls-Royce of Austria' was made for a small and esoteric clientele which had included the last two Hapsburg Emperors. Though aggressive vee radiators were used in the early 1920s, latter-day Gräf *und* Stifts were handsome, well-proportioned cars wearing silver lion mascots on their filler caps. Their luxury models were invariably enormous, notably a pair of 7·7-litre sixes, the s.v. SR1 and the pushrod SR4, which acquired four-wheel brakes in 1923. Chain-driven o.h.c., made their appearance in 1928 on two new and more modestly-dimensioned sixes, the 4-litre S4 and the 7·1-litre SP7, these evolving into a range which continued until the end of private-car production in 1938.

Both the 5·9-litre straight-eight SP8 and its companion six, the SP5, retained upstairs camshafts, together with blocks of silumin alloy, dual-choke carburetters fed by electric pump, hydraulic brakes, and semi-elliptic springing assisted by hydraulic dampers. The SP8's four-speed synchromesh gearbox had an overdrive top gear; vacuum-servo assistance was furnished for gear changing as well as for the brakes. Other refinements embraced thermostatically-controlled radiator shutters and centralized chassis lubrication. The 148-inch wheelbase chassis carried some superb coachwork by Viennese houses such as Armbruster and Keibl; the average weight of a limousine was in the region of 5,500 pounds.

Gräf *und* Stift were, however, primarily interested in trucks, and very few SP8s were made; by 1934 such private-car production as there was centred round local versions of the rear-wheel-drive 15CV Citroën (Type MF6), later supplanted as a cheap line by the Ford V8 (Gräfford). Both wore their silver lions apologetically. There were also a couple of interesting prototypes, the G36 and the C12. The former was a straight-eight of 78 × 121 mm (4·7 litres) which developed 110 b.h.p. as against the SP8's 125, while the C12 was a small 3·9-litre V-12 which marked a reversion to side valves. At the same time a handful of SP8s were made with redesigned radiator grilles under the designation SP9. Gräf *und* Stift are still active as manufacturers of heavy diesel trucks and buses.

43 FORD V8 MODEL-18, 1932, USA

Ford's Model-A of 1927 was a real step forward after nineteen years of Model-

T, but it was still only a four in an era of growing multi-cylinderism. Yet Henry Ford's rooted aversion to sixes was to lead, four years later, to a revolution in casting techniques. At long last ways had been found to make a really cheap V8 in vast quantities, with integral cast-iron block and crankcase, and aluminium pistons. The new engine had its two banks of cylinders set at 90 degrees; a helical gear drive 20 inches long drove the camshaft without any intervening idler gears or timing chains, cylinder heads were detachable, and there were twin water pumps. Other refinements included a three-speed synchromesh gearbox, rubber insulation between frame and axles, and safety glass all round on *de luxe* models.

The rest of it was interchangeable with the four-cylinder Model-B, itself an up-rated A. Lubrication was still pressure-and-splash, the mechanical brakes were designed to stop a 65 m.p.h. motor-car, Ford's antiquated transverse springing was retained, and the frame with its three cross-members was given no serious reinforcement. The splendours of such a formula were sizzling performance and acceleration; though at first only 65 b.h.p. were claimed from the 3·6-litre engine, the V8 was compact, on a 106-inch wheelbase, and light (a cabriolet turned the scales at only 2,576 pounds). Hence it would exceed 75 m.p.h. on a 4·33:1 top gear, and accelerate to 60 m.p.h. in 16·8 seconds, something that few thoroughbred sports cars could manage. Steering was high-geared, but for all that the V8 was lethal in unskilled hands, which explains why the 1933 Model-40s had some much-needed cruciform bracing for their frames, not to mention an extra six inches of wheelbase.

In spite of this, the car was an instant success. Gangsters (Clyde Barrow, John Dillinger) loved it, and so did British rallyists (though an RAC rating of 30 h.p. limited Dagenham's production of Model-18 to 911 units, and obliged the British factory to carry the original V8 over into a second season). At a starting price of $460 (£92) the V8 cost only fifty dollars more than a Model-B, and helped Ford to sell 298,647 in 1932 alone; the 15 m.p.g. thirst hardly mattered in a land of cheap fuel.

In addition to straightforward foreign assembly, V8s were made in Britain, France (Matford), Germany, Hungary (Mavag) and Austria (Gräfford). The engine was also standardized by Chenard-Walcker in France and by Jensen and Allard in Britain, while V8s of one type and another served on both sides (and pretty well every front) in World War II. Among less likely applications were in Bren-gun carriers and as power for the mine-exploders carried by the Wellington bombers of RAF Coastal Command. America's last flathead V8 engines were made in 1953, but the unit survived for another two or three years in the British company's trucks.

44 GRAHAM BLUE STREAK, 1932; CUSTOM SUPER-CHARGER EIGHT, 1934, USA

Once the stylist took over in America, periodic trend-setters emerged. Graham's 1932 Eight was to influence the majority of the nation's manufacturers in 1933 and 1934. Its principal innovation was, of course, the use of fender skirts, but the shallow windscreen and windows, plus the application of the compound curve, were also characteristics of a shape duly copied by Ford and Continental among others. The Graham's influence was extended into the nursery through the medium of Tootsie Toys, whose realistic rubber-tyred miniature 'Grahams' included variations (a town car, for instance) never contemplated by the Graham Brothers.

Mechanically, the Blue Streak was less sensational, if one excepts the achievement of a low body line by making the rear axle pass through the chassis side-members. The five-bearing 4-litre straight-eight engine developed an average 90 b.h.p., and differed from routine practice only in its corrosion-prone alloy head; though allegedly of Graham's own make it was at least sixty per cent Continental. The three-speed synchromesh gearbox incorporated a free wheel, and brakes were hydraulic. Wheelbase was 123 inches, and top speed in the region of 80 m.p.h. A similarly-styled six followed in 1933.

Sales were, however, discouraging: 12,970 in 1932, with a drop of 2,000 in 1933; but in 1934 the firm offered an aircraft-type centrifugal supercharger, driven off the water pump shaft and running at five times engine speed. Such extra urge was reserved for the relatively expensive Custom Eight, which also had downdraught carburation and a 'two-stage' accelerator pedal à la Mercedes-Benz. Output went up to 135 b.h.p., and top speed to well over 90 m.p.h., with an 0–50 acceleration time of 13 seconds. The frame was now fully cruciform-braced, and other improvements included the fashionable no-draught ventilation. Eight-cylinder prices ranged from a low $975 (£195) for the standard unblown business coupé, up to $1,330 (£260) for the supercharged trunk sedan. Britons paid £565 for the latter type.

Unfortunately, too many people preferred established automobiles like the newly redesigned Buick NA series. Graham gained precious few customers, and though the blown eights continued into 1935 with pedal starting, their narrow grilles and beaver tails reflected the influence of the previous season's La Salle (45). Subsequent supercharged Grahams used the 3½-litre six-cylinder engine.

45 **LA SALLE,** 1932, 1934, USA

Conceived by General Motors to bridge the gap between Cadillac and Buick, the Cadillac-built La Salle was Harley Earl's (and the American industry's) first organized exercise in styling.

The original La Salles, which appeared in 1927, were really compact Cadillacs; cylinder capacity of the side-valve vee-eight engine was 303 cu. in. (5 litres) as against Cadillac's 341, side-by-side connecting-rods replaced the Cadillac's forked ones, and the standard wheelbase was a modest 125 inches. The result was not only handsome, with overtones of Hispano-Suiza; it was good for 80 m.p.h. on 75–80 b.h.p., and could be bought for less than $3,000 (£600). First season's sales were an encouraging 27,000, and in 1929 La Salle shared one of Cadillac's most important innovations, the silent synchromesh gearbox. But though quality was maintained, the *marque* was fast losing its *cachet*, largely thanks to economies imposed by the Depression. There was only six inches difference between Cadillac and La Salle wheelbases in 1930, and a year later both breeds shared the same 115 b.h.p. 5·8-litre engine, with a basic price differential of a mere $400. 1932 La Salles had servo-assisted clutches, free wheels, and mechanical pump feed; servo brakes followed on the beautiful 1933s with vee-grilles and fender skirts à la Graham (44), but in a declining market Cadillacs outsold La Salles two to one, and halfway through the year production of the latter make was halted.

For the 1934 revival, Cadillac 'downrated' their companion car, though they also created a style-leader that took over where Graham had left off. The narrow radiator grille, pontoon-shaped fenders, 'turret top' all-steel body, bullet-shaped headlamps attached to the grille, and thin-section double-bar bumpers all had their imitators. The portholes in the hood were, amusingly, to become a Buick hallmark some fifteen years later, while the disc 'wheels' were in fact clip-ons concealing mundane pressed-steel artilleries.

Mechanics were more pedestrian; for in place of the vee-eight was a 3·8-litre five-bearing straight-eight derived from the contemporary Oldsmobile. Other Oldsmobile heritages were the coil-spring i.f.s., the cruciform-braced frame, and the hydraulic brakes (GM's first). Oddly, this pooling of ideas did not include parts interchangeability; Oldsmobile pistons, bearings and carburetters would not fit a La Salle! Though shorter, with a wheelbase of 119 inches, lighter (by some 900 pounds) and a great deal cheaper ($1,595, or £725 in England) than the classic La Salles, the straight-eight was no best-seller, even after a convertible had been chosen as the 1934 Indianapolis pace-car. By 1937, La Salle were back with a vee-eight again.

46 AUSTIN TEN-FOUR,
1932, 1934, Great Britain

One of the recipes of Herbert Austin's success was that for all his conservatism, he invariably kept a best-seller in his catalogues. In 1932, when the Seven was beginning to suffer seriously from adipose tissue, he came up with a Family Ten—what is more, he had it in quantity production before either Morris or Hillman, even if the latter's Minx (78) had been at the 1931 Show. Results were impressive: 8,200 cars delivered between May and December, 1932, 21,200 in 1933, 25,000 in 1934, 27,500 in 1935, and 28,500 in 1936, the last season of 'sit-up-and-beg' styling. Though completely modernized for 1937, and once again in 1939, the Ten was destined to remain in continuous production (thanks to the wartime 'Tillies') until superseded by the o.h.v. A40 at the end of 1947.

The vehicle as originally marketed at £168 ($840) in sedan form was conventional in the best Austin sense. Its 1,125 cc side-valve four-cylinder engine developed a sedate 21 b.h.p., and was fed by mechanical pump from a six-gallon rear tank. Cooling was by thermosyphon, there was 6-volt coil ignition, and the usual four-speed gearbox with its long and whippy central lever had low and wide ratios, and a slow change. The cable-operated four-wheel brakes were actuated by pedal and lever, and the car had compact dimensions; overall length was only 130 inches. The instruments were grouped in front of the driver (with a generous glove locker on the other side) and the Ten was cheap to run (34 m.p.g.) as well as reliable. By 1933 the range had been extended to embrace open two-seater, tourer, delivery van, and even roll-top cabriolet versions, while for the first three seasons styling hardly changed; 1934s, however, had 12-volt electrics, synchromesh on top and third, turn indicators, and cruciform-braced frames.

1935 saw some serious styling alterations; the traditional chromium-plated radiator shell gave way to a rounded grille, while the four-window sedan body (and cabriolets and tourers as well) acquired small rear boots, full of spare wheel. Other refinements included a synchromesh second gear and concealed turn indicators. Interestingly, the Ten was chosen for Austin's first experiments in modern shapes; at the beginning of the season a semi-streamlined six-window sedan was introduced, this Sherborne paving the way for the Cambridge of 1937.

47 PANHARD 6CS 13CV,
1932, France

Panhard were among the most devoted advocates of the Knight double-sleeve-valve engine, adopted in 1911 and standardized by them from 1923 to the outbreak of World War II.

In the inter-war era their products were stolid, beautifully-made and conservative in style and specification. A six did not reappear in the range until the 1926 Salon, when the 16CV X57 was offered in chassis form at £800 ($4,000). This was a big car with a 3·4-litre engine and a 138-inch wheelbase, in spite of which it would do 75 m.p.h.

By 1928 the smaller 1·8-litre X59, rated at 10CV, had joined it; though this retained magneto ignition, it had twin carburetters and quarter-elliptic rear springs. The range was rounded out in 1929 with a 12–14CV (sold as the 18–50 h.p. in Britain), closely based on the 10CV, with the same four-bearing engine, carburation, alloy pistons, wet-plate clutch, and four-speed silent third gearbox with a peculiar X-gate. (On Panhards, first and fourth were on the left, and the two intermediate ratios on the right. RHD was, of course standard). Bodies usually took the form of square-rigged fabric sedans with rear trunks; the 12–14CV was a heavy car at 3,024 pounds, and its wood artillery wheels made it look heavier.

An improved chassis featured on the 6CS of 1931; this was of platform type, covered over in sheet metal with wells for the passengers' feet. Rear springs were now semi-elliptic, and Panhard dispensed with shock absorbers at the rear; instead, they fitted adjustable clamping bolts to the springs. Another absentee was the oil pressure gauge, for on Panhards the ignition automatically cut when pressure fell below a safe level. Retained were the powerful four-wheel internal-expanding brakes, and more elegant coachbuilt bodies replaced the old fabric type. In addition to the basic 13CV there were the more potent 2,516 cc 6CSZ and the long-wheelbase 3½-litre 6DS for seven-seater coachwork, which weighed around two tons, but would top the 70 m.p.h. mark.

By 1934 Panhard's refinements included automatic clutches and free wheels. An interesting novelty was the 'Panoramique' body on which the screen pillars were split, with curved glass inserts, to give extra vision, and the cars continued unchanged until the advent of the astonishing and hideous Dynamic in 1937. They were delightful to drive, but at 49,000 francs the 6DS was no bargain, and an under-employed factory gave the lie to *'les raffinements mécaniques de la voiture de demain'* energetically promoted by André Kow in the company's display advertising of the period.

48 GOLIATH DREIRADWAGEN, 1932, Germany

Weimar Germany, like France, offered some loopholes in its laws calculated to appeal to the marginal motorist. Owners of cars of under 200 cc were exempt, not only from circulation tax, but from the need for a driving licence. Hence the cyclecar was able to survive, often in alarming manifestations such as the Framo, which perpetuated the Phänomobil idea of mounting the entire power pack over the driven front wheel. Even a list price of £40 ($200) could not make this solution attractive. The Goliath, the first automobile venture of Carl Borgward, was more successful. He had started by making radiators in 1921, progressing three years later to motorcycles (under the Lloyd-Fix name) and tri-vans. He was not to gain complete control of the Hansa firm until 1932.

His private car model, the Goliath Pionier, was unveiled at the 1928 Berlin Show and was produced until 1933. The ingredients were simple; a rudimentary chassis (to which some equally simple cruciform bracing was subsequently added), in the rear of which was mounted a 198 cc air-cooled, single-cylinder, two-stroke Ilo engine, in unit with a three-speed-and-reverse-gearbox. This unit drove the rear wheels through articulated shafts, while the single front wheel was supported on one side only to facilitate wheel-changing. Brakes were uncoupled; unlike the Framo and some other contemporaries, the Goliath had car-type controls, and the bodies—a roadster and a fixed-head coupé—were quite elegant as well as compact. Contemporary publicity pictures showed a *hausfrau* and her two children squeezed into the coupé's rumble seat, but it is questionable whether the Goliath could have coped with such a load. As it was, maximum speed was a sedate 35 m.p.h., for a fuel consumption of 65 m.p.g. During the last three years of production four thousand were sold. Thereafter vans of similar type were made until the collapse of the Borgward empire in 1961.

Borgward also tried his hand in 1933 with a four-wheeled Hansa minicar. This was a would-be rival for the D.K.W., with backbone frame, all-independent springing and fabric-covered aerodynamic sedan coachwork. The engine, a 400 cc vertical-twin two-stroke, was fitted at the rear: it was prone to seizures and (on occasion) to self-incandescence as well. It lasted only two seasons. Borgward was to return to minimal two-strokes in 1950 with the 10 b.h.p., 293 cc Lloyd, called by its compatriots 'The Elastoplast Car'. By now the traditional wood-and-fabric construction had been ousted by plastic materials.

49 MINERVA AP 22CV, 1932, 1934, Belgium

Minerva of Antwerp were feeling the cold worse than most makers of luxury carriages. The emphasis had always been on the formal and chauffeur-driven vehicle, and, despite a useful American connection, most customers had come from Britain. Already in 1927 the company had sought to widen the product's appeal with a medium-priced 2-litre 12CV six, retaining, of course, the Knight sleeve-valve engine. Two years later came the most glamorous of all the Minervas, the vast 6·6-litre 40CV Type-AL, a two-and-a-half tonner on a 153½-in. wheelbase, for which Britons and Americans alike paid the equivalent of $12,000. This one appeared at the 1929 London and Paris Shows, but by the time the Brussels Salon came round they had produced a more modest eight, the 3,958 cc AP.

Its nine-bearing sleeve-valve engine was fed by electric pump from an 18-gallon rear tank, coil ignition only was provided, and the power unit rode on rubber. The single-plate clutch and four-speed silent-third gearbox were conventional enough, semi-elliptic springs were used all round, and the brakes had Dewandre servo assistance. The generous 144-inch wheelbase made the AP ideal for chauffeur-driven bodies such as Minerva's own stately seven-seater limousine, though such Belgian coachbuilders as D'Ieteren and Vanden Plas produced some handsome convertibles on the short, 130-inch chassis, and by 1932 a sports model with twin oil pumps and fifteen more brake horses was listed.

For all its stateliness the AP was a respectable performer. A prototype with two-door sedan bodywork averaged nearly 50 m.p.h. between Marseilles and Ostend, and a 2¼-ton limousine would easily top the 70 mark, with a useful 65 available in the high third. A British report described the car as 'as easy to handle as many vehicles of half the size'. Unfortunately owners in quest of seven seats could buy something cheaper and simpler to maintain from firms such as Fiat, Renault, and Austin, who charged less than £600. The Minerva cost £975 in England. 1932 saw the AR, which was really a short-chassis AP with two less cylinders, but Minerva were on their way out. An uninteresting sleeve-valve 2-litre four, the M4, was tried in 1934, but fared even worse than the last F.N.s.

Production had virtually ceased by 1936. Until the middle 1950s APs and ARs were still to be seen earning their keep on wedding and funeral hire in Flanders; some operators, however, preferred second-hand Dodge engines to the complexities and dipsomaniac thirst of elderly Knights.

50 FRANKLIN SERIES-17, 1933, USA

Not all American manufacturers were committed to the stereotyped formula of six or eight vertical cylinders, pump circulation, side valves, three speeds, and a strictly orthodox chassis. Among the more seasoned heretics was Herbert H. Franklin of Syracuse, N.Y., who had been building air-cooled cars since 1901, and even in 1927 was quite happy with a 3·3-litre six that was by no means as ordinary as it looked. The full-elliptic springs conferred an excellent ride, the wooden chassis frame saved weight, and rear-wheel and transmission brakes sufficed. By 1932 its successor, the Airman Six, was a rather expensive 4½-litre with orthodox chassis, more adequate anchors, and synchromesh (introduced during 1929, close behind Cadillac). Only the full-elliptic suspension and the air cooling remained as reminders of more individualistic days when sales were five times the paltry 1,975 units of this Depression year.

Franklin had been planning their V-12 since 1928, with the aid of Glenn Shoemaker, an engineer from the U.S.A.A.F.'s McCook Field. Further, they had borrowed five million dollars to back the venture, which might have succeeded but for the slump. By 1932 the company was bankrupt, and the nascent Series-17 became a cost accountant's automobile.

What had been intended as a fairly compact two-tonner on a 137-inch wheelbase emerged as a 144-inch monster weighing close on three tons. Franklin's traditional weight-savers—the tubular front axle, the full-elliptic springs, and the alloy differential housing—were discarded in favour of an orthodox frame riding on semi-elliptics and proprietary axles. Various engine sizes were proposed, including a 544 cu. in. (9-litre) giant, before the company settled for a 6·6-litre unit which developed 150 b.h.p. at 3,100 r.p.m. This was described as 'supercharged', but this publicity jargon referred to simple, driver-controlled ducts from the air-cooling chamber to the carburetter. Other features followed accepted big-car practice: mechanical pump feed, a twin-plate clutch, and hydraulic brakes. A Columbia two-speed rear axle was standard equipment; this gave a high top of 3·4:1, enabling the car to cruise indefinitely at 70 m.p.h. The elegant bodies and vee-grille had a hint of Graham, but were in fact based on rejected studies made by Le Baron for Lincoln.

The Franklin Twelve came too late. After the first season, prices were slashed, from $4,400 (£890) to $2,885

(£575), but only 200 were made. Some had odd fates. A specially lengthened 161-inch chassis was commissioned by a Long Island undertaker, and at least one Series-17 engine found its way into an early Lincoln Continental as a replacement for the unreliable Zephyr unit.

51 LANCIA AUGUSTA,
1933, 1935, Italy

One of the nicest small cars to come out of the Depression years was the Augusta. Its appearance was homely, its performance unspectacular (70 m.p.h. was hard work), and it lacked the now generally accepted synchromesh, even if, in the words of one enthusiastic journalist, 'the gears almost fall in'. It did, however, have hydraulic brakes, and energetic trials up and down Turin's notorious Superga Hill had convinced Vincenzo Lancia that the correct answer to fade was a combination of finned drums and unpolished surfaces.

The rest of the car followed the classic Lancia formula. The engine was a narrow-angle, short-stroke V4 with roller-chain drive for its overhead camshaft; this took up little room and permitted comfortable four-seater bodywork on a vehicle only 153 inches long. Output was 35 b.h.p. at 4,000 r.p.m., but it could withstand sustained high revs. It was mounted in unit with a single-plate clutch and a four-speed silent-third gearbox; a free wheel was standard equipment. Ignition was by coil, and the Zenith carburetter was fed by gravity. Inevitably Lancia's traditional sliding-pillar i.f.s., dating back to the first Lambda of 1922, was retained, and there was a reversion to full unitary construction on the standard four-door pillarless sedan, which weighed 1,850 pounds, and cost £390 ($1,960) in Britain. As in the case of the early Lambdas, Lancia marketed a separate platform chassis for special bodies; this one had a rear tank and electric pump feed.

The Augusta could put up excellent average speeds, and among satisfied customers was Tazio Nuvolari. In England, the Duke of Richmond and Gordon fitted a chassis version with Italianate four-seater sports tourer body and Centric supercharger, in which form the car was persuaded to do 75 m.p.h., and accelerate to 60 m.p.h. in 25 seconds. Augustas were also made in France (only blocks and heads were imported), and 2,500 of these 'Belnas' found buyers between 1933 and 1936 at a price (28,500 francs) modest enough to compete with the more stolid 1½-litre products of the native industry, if not with the rising star of Citroën's still temperamental *traction*. 1934 and later Augusta *de luxe* models had slightly vee'd radiators and centre-lock wheels in place of the bolt-on type. Production ended in 1936, when the Augusta gave way to Vincenzo Lancia's swansong, the brilliant 1,352 cc Aprilia. He died before this one reached the public in any quantity.

52 DE SOTO AIRFLOW SE, 1934, USA

Chrysler's Airflows, the creation of Carl Breer, have gone down in history as the most appalling stylistic solecisms of all time. It is, however, a matter of opinion whether they arrived before their time, or would have been inacceptable in any era.

Airflows were said to pitch deplorably, despite an excellent basic ride obtained by mounting the engine twenty inches over the front axle, thus dispensing with the need for i.f.s., a configuration which American engineers had yet to master in 1934. There was no external luggage access (a failing by no means peculiar to Chrysler products), and such under-hood complexities as laterally-mounted header tanks had their miseries. Access to the valves was gained by first removing a wheel and its housing. Sales were depressing; 13,940 De Sotos and 11,292 Chryslers in the first season, with a steady drop to 4,600 in 1937, the Airflow's final year. The Corporation, who had started off bravely with a wide range extending from the SE De Soto Six at $995 (£200) to the monstrous 146½-inch Chrysler Custom Imperial at $5,000 (£1,000), could indeed be thankful that they had kept the Dodge and Plymouth lines free from Mr Breer's aerodynamic concepts.

What emerged from copious wind-tunnel testing was a semi-unitary welded-steel teardrop structure with slab sides, an alligator hood, and faired-in headlamps, crowned by an outrageous waterfall grille. Beneath it were the usual stock Chrysler mechanics, which included three forward speeds, hydraulic brakes, semi-elliptic springs, and a spiral bevel rear axle; hypoid final drive came on the 1935s. The rear wheels were spatted.

De Soto's version came on a 115½-inch wheelbase, and its 3,956 cc 95 b.h.p. engine was the only six in the Airflow range. Overdrive, standard on the costlier Chryslers, was an optional extra, and the car weighed 3,570 pounds, giving it a top speed of around 85 m.p.h. An example collected a string of A.A.A. Stock-Car Records, averaging 76·2 m.p.h. for 500 miles, while another SE turned in a mean 21·4 m.p.g. on a trans-continental drive from New York to San Francisco.

In England the SE went under the name of 'Chrysler Croydon Airflow Six', and sold for £499. 1935 Airflows were revised with new 'widow's peak' grilles, but the nominal SGs sold by Chrysler's Kew branch were in fact existing SEs to which the latest hood assembly had been hurriedly tacked on. Some of these unsold stocks, indeed, turned up a year later as 1936-model S2s! But by this time De Soto's Airflow sales were down to the 5,000 level, and in 1937 only the eight-cylinder Chrysler species was offered. The addition of a 1937 Imperial hood at one end, and a built-out trunk at the other had destroyed the purity of the original shape, such as it was, and these C17s were the last of the line.

53 J.M.B., 1934, 1935, Great Britain

British three-wheeler design alternated between the car on three wheels (B.S.A.) or the hairy sporting device for graduate motorcyclists (Morgan). Pure utility was seldom studied after the demise of the basic two-speed Morgan theme. Thus it was a brave gesture on the part of Messrs. Jones, Mason and Barrow of Ringwood to seek a civilized alternative to the motorcycle combination.

What they produced in 1933 was a simple unitary structure with ash planks as body supports; the engine and transmission had their own separate tubular frame. The mechanics consisted of a 500 cc single-cylinder s.v. J.A.P. engine mounted horizontally behind the seats, and transmitting its power *via* a three-speed-and-reverse Albion motorcycle gearbox to the single, chain-driven rear wheel. Ignition was by coil, the front wheels were independently sprung, and brakes were of three-wheel, coupled type. Controls followed car lines with three pedals. The appearance was similarly orthodox, with a dummy hood housing the fuel tank, and crowned with a Singer-shaped 'radiator'. The chain steering gear and the external kick-starter were legacies from the cyclecar. The standard body was a fabric-covered occasional four-seater with only one door. Weight was kept low, at 624 pounds in road trim, and on 14 b.h.p. the J.M.B. would do 50 m.p.h., as well as recording a frugal 71 m.p.g.

Unfortunately the sponsors listened to their dealers' demand for something more car-like, and the 1935 Mustang series came out with a separate steel-tube chassis and steel-panelled bodywork. This was admittedly handsome; it was also quite rapid when fitted with the optional 21 b.h.p. o.h.v. engine, but it was strictly a two-seater, it was more complicated, and also more expensive (£91 as against £74). A 2 + 2 aerodynamic sports sedan was displayed at the 1934 Motorcycle Show, but never saw production. Before 1935 was out J.M.B. Motors had closed down; not, however, before G. H. Jones had built and tested a utility prototype which would have cost £41 to make, and could thus have been marketed at a bargain £65. This reverted to 1934 lines, but used a 348 cc two-stroke Villiers engine; it was tried in three- and four-wheeler forms. Between 200 and 250 J.M.B.s were built, and to this day it has the distinction of being the only make of car produced in the New Forest.

54 ROVER 14, 1935, 1936, Great Britain

The Rover Fourteen not only represents the British middle-class family car at its best but is also a classic example of how something cheap and nasty can be developed into a quality machine, which with the rest of the series was selling at the rate of 12,000 a year by 1938.

The genesis of the model came in 1932, when Rover were still interested in cheap family machinery. The original Pilot was yet another variation on the Wolseley Hornet-Triumph Scorpion theme, using as its basis the undistinguished worm-driven Rover Ten with quarter-elliptic rear springing. To these elements was added a 1,410 cc six-cylinder pushrod engine developing 30 b.h.p., fed by mechanical pump from a rear tank. The combination of a four-speed silent-third gearbox and a 5·4:1 back axle resulted in the usual refined gutlessness. A standard sedan cost only £219 ($1,095) but Rover offered a wide range of custom bodies by approved coachbuilders.

1933 Pilots had 1·6-litre engines, hydraulic brakes, and the free wheel, a Rover feature until the middle fifties. The price was up to £258, and there was also a companion Speed Model with triple-carburetter, 54 b.h.p. unit in an underslung frame. This last was standardized in 1934 along with spiral bevel final drive and Startix automatic starters (a short-lived fad). The wheelbase was lengthened to 112 ins., and the bodies were now lower and better-proportioned. A harmonic stabilizer was built into the front bumper; though Rover used a remote-control gear lever; this was bolted direct to the frame, so eliminating the woolly feel of many such linkages. Other pleasing details were the automatic chassis lubrication standardized in 1935, and the handsome instrument panels with under-hood access to the wiring.

Specification remained orthodox, with beam axles and hydraulic dampers, though there were some experiments with i.f.s. in 1934. In stock form a 14 weighed just over 2,900 pounds, returning 70 m.p.h. and 21-23 m.p.g., though for the more enthusiastic driver there was still a three-carburetter sporting variant with electric pump feed, identifiable by its centre-lock wire wheels and cross-braced headlamps. This was usually fitted with fastback four-door 'coupé' bodywork, and was good for 80 m.p.h. 1936 Rovers had Girling mechanical brakes, but were otherwise unchanged. A complete redesign was undertaken for 1937, and the Fourteen survived with some seasonal changes until the end of 1947.

55 TATRA 77, 1935, Czechoslovakia

Hans Ledwinka's Tatras had long been renowned for advanced ideas. His small cars used air-cooled, horizontally-opposed engines, backbone frames, and all-independent suspension by transverse leaf springs. Even the bigger, water-cooled species retained the sophisticated chassis. But the Type 77 unveiled at the 1934 Berlin Show was a sensation, if only because no publicity had been given to Ledwinka's first rear-engined experiment, the little aerodynamic twin-cylinder V750 of 1932.

As before, all four wheels were

independently sprung, but the traditional Tatra backbone was now reinforced by a platform for the body; at the rear of this structure lived a 3-litre o.h.v. air-cooled vee-eight engine developing 60 b.h.p. at 3,500 r.p.m. There were twin fans, and the twin Zenith carburetters were fed from a tank mounted amidships. The engine, four-speed synchromesh gearbox and final drive unit were removable for easy servicing, and other features included centralized chassis lubrication and hydraulic brakes. The body was a fully aerodynamic six-seater on a wooden frame, with wrap-round windscreen and central driving position. The luggage was housed beneath the rear seats, while the short hood accommodated two spare wheels. Despite a modest output and a weight of 3,750 pounds, the Tatra's superior aerodynamics gave it a top speed of 90–95 m.p.h. To its credit there was superb suspension: a 77 could be driven fast with two wheels on the kerb. On the debit side were non-existent rearward vision, a sloppy gear-change, and a sudden, vicious breakaway point.

Production models had conventional r.h.d., and during 1935 the 77 gave way to the 77a with 3,380 cc, 75 b.h.p. engine. In 1936 came the 87, which marked a reversion to three litres, but was the fastest of the family, thanks to a shorter wheelbase of only 112 inches and a saving of some 600 pounds in weight. This one had a single carburetter, and was identifiable by its

tail fin. The equipment included a radio, a sliding roof and seats convertible into a bed. Pre-war production amounted to 105 77s, 150 77a's, and 2,307 87s, while another 1,721 of this last-mentioned type were turned out between 1946 and 1948. Thereafter the company, now state-controlled, devoted their energy to a 2-litre flat-four based on the 1938 T.97 prototype. They did not revert to the vee-eight configuration until 1955, with the T.603 series.

56 DATSUN, 1935, 1937, Japan

The original Datsun is often regarded as a direct crib of the Austin Seven. Herbert Austin, in fact, imported one from Australia for study (it still exists in England) and decided that there were no grounds for legal action. The main difference between English and Japanese idioms lay in the latter's worm-drive rear axle and semi-elliptic rear springs, though both cars used transverse-leaf suspension at the front.

Built in conformity with the restrictive Automobile Control Laws of Japan, the first Datson (i.e. 'son of D.A.T.') of 1932 was a true miniature with a wheelbase of 74 ins. and a track of only 39 ins. In general layout it followed Austin lines, with a 54 × 54 mm. (495 cc) side-valve four-cylinder engine, 6-volt coil ignition, single-plate clutch, and three-speed gearbox. Output was 10 b.h.p., and top speed 45 m.p.h. Home-market buyers paid the equivalent of £140 ($700); in addition to the regular roadsters and coupés there were some single-seater models to take advantage of a tax loophole. By 1934 the cars had become Datsuns; 1935 and later types ran to 722 cc and 16 b.h.p., with wheelbases five inches longer. The weight was now 1,300 pounds, and four-seater bodywork was available, necessitating an abysmal 6·5:1 top gear admirably suited to Japan's tortuous road system.

Production was never substantial. In 1937 Nissan Motors spoke of an annual output of 15,000 Datsuns plus 3,000 'large cars' (i.e. their version of the Graham Six), but it is unlikely if anything like this quantity was ever released for civilian consumption. Nor was Japan a serious exporter. A few Datsuns found their way to other Far Eastern countries, and in 1934 a trial batch of three dozen chassis was sent to Australia, where they were fitted with locally-built sedan and tourer bodies. They failed to impress.

The old-school Datsuns were revived after the War, and both standard and de luxe models were catalogued in 1950. The former was indistinguishable from a 1938, but the latter's styling aped that of the latest American Crosley. Capacity went up from 722 cc to 860 cc in 1952, by which time Datsuns had piston-type shock absorbers, hydraulic brakes, and an 84-inch wheelbase which rendered four-door bodywork viable. Also in the range was a sports two-seater with hand-made bodywork in the M.G. idiom. Such traditional vehicles, now with hypoid final drive and semi-elliptics at the rear, were still being made in 1959.

57 BUICK SERIES-40, 1936, USA

Buick, 'the Doctor's Friend', has long had a solid hold on the American middle-class market. Throughout the inter-war years, the *marque* was never out of the nation's Top Ten, even in 1933, when sales nose-dived to a miserable 40,620. Buick's progress in the early 1930s typifies the attitude of a middle-class maker in an uneasy era. 1929–30 had seen an abortive, cheap companion make, the Marquette (like the 1934 La Salle, it was largely Oldsmobile). Straight-eights, synchromesh and all-expanding brakes had been 1931's innovations, followed by mechanical pump feed and 'Wizard Control' (which meant a free wheel and a vacuum-operated clutch) in 1932. These were followed by cruciform-braced frames and no-draught ventilation in 1933, and alloy pistons, pedal-operated starters, and the notorious 'Knee Action' i.f.s. in 1934. In 1935 Buick virtually marked time during a $15,000,000 refit at the factory, but 1936 was a boom year, with 179,533 cars sold.

The cars were o.h.v. straight-eights with five main bearings, coil ignition, and dual-choke downdraught carburetters. There was synchromesh on the two upper ratios of the three-speed gearbox; the only mechanical novelty of the season was the adoption of hydraulic brakes, with an umbrella-handle handbrake working on the rear wheels only, but stylewise the Buick was all-new. The curved fencer's-mask grille no longer pretended to be a radiator, and the all-steel 'turret-top' body pioneered by La Salle (45) in 1934 was now standardized throughout the native General Motors range. Buick sedans had integral boots roomy enough for 'two teenagers and a Great Dane'. The 'snob' dual sidemounts lived in cellulosed covers, wheels were of the pressed-steel spoked type and even ashtray lids followed the shape of the grille. The domestic Buick featured eighteen models, with two engine options (3·8 and 5·2 litres) and four wheelbase lengths. Prices ranged from $765 to $1,945 (£153–£390), which overlapped with Chevrolet at one end, and with Cadillac at the other. Britons (whose Buicks were 'Empire-built' in the McLaughlin plant at Oshawa, Ontario) paid £455 for a stock 40.

The 40 was the cheapest and best-selling Buick. No model retailed for more than $900 and it accounted for more than 75 per cent of the year's sales. The wheelbase was a compact 118 ins., a sedan weighed 3,360 pounds, and on an output of 93 b.h.p., top speed was just over 80 m.p.h., with an 0–50 m.p.h. acceleration time in the region of 12 seconds. Fuel consumption was 18 m.p.g. Interestingly, 1938 editions of the 40 were to be available with G.M.'s first easy-change gearbox,

a four-speed semi-automatic made by Buick for Oldsmobile.

58 LINCOLN-ZEPHYR, 1936, 1937, USA

The fastback Zephyr was one of the sensations of the 1936 New York Show. It set no price records for Twelves, even at $1,300 (£480 in London), for Auburn had already marketed a V-12 at an incredible $975 way back in 1932. What it did have was a streamlined teardrop shape, an alligator hood and unitary construction, the fruit of lengthy experiments conducted by John Tjaarda with rear-engined aerodynamic prototypes using Ford V8 engines; these power units proved inadequate, though one of Tjaarda's cars managed 110 m.p.h.

As 'productionized' by Frank Johnson, the Zephyr was front-engined. It also acquired such inevitable Ford features as beam axles, transverse springs, and cable-operated brakes, but its 4·4-litre engine developed a useful 110 b.h.p., and in its 4·33:1 top gear the car could not only attain 90 m.p.h., but also climb a 1-in-6½ hill. The wheelbase was a modest 122 in., but a generous overhang at either end gave it an impressive overall length of 202 in. Headlamps were streamlined into the front wings. The price of this shape was deplorable rearward vision, but the Zephyr was well received, especially in Britain, where its outstanding looks and flexibility were perhaps less important than its frugal appetite for fuel. 20 m.p.g. was quite possible, some compensation for an annual tax of £46.25 by 1939!

Unfortunately the Lincoln image demanded twelve cylinders. At the same time the Zephyr's middle-class status demanded that the mechanics should incorporate a high proportion of stock Ford parts, to enable the cars to be serviced by Ford dealers. These folk could not cope; hence the model soon acquired its unhappy reputation for short engine life. On the credit side, the Zephyr's annual sales were steady around the 20,000 mark during a run which continued until Pearl Harbor, and was resumed after 1945, although the Zephyr name was not used on post-war developments.

Later improvements included a longer wheelbase, hydraulic tappets, a dashboard change, and a neater fleur-de-lys grille in 1938 and some much-needed hydraulic braking in 1939. 1940 cars had more powerful 4·8-litre engines, power windows and seat adjustment and column change, while 1941's were available with overdrive, and 1942's with the troublesome Liquamatic automatic gearbox.

Those who dismiss the Zephyr as gutless and unreliable should remember that it made Lincoln the world's largest-ever producer of Twelves (well over 150,000 of all types between 1932 and 1948); formed the basis for the glamorous and much-collected Continental coupés and cabriolets created by Edsel Ford in 1939; and also powered several interesting British sporting cars, notably the Allard and the Atalanta.

59 **FORD TEN,** 1936, 1938, Great Britain

Ford's European operations gained a great fillip in 1932 with the advent of their first European-type small car, the 933 cc Model-Y, made in Germany and France as well as in Britain. Though this became the first full-sized sedan to be sold in this country for £100 ($500), the Model-C Ten of 1935 is almost more important, especially to the sporting fraternity, who owe to its simple mechanics two generations of home-brewed 'special'.

Unveiled at London's Albert Hall in October, 1934, the Model-C resembled the new 1935 American V8 in miniature. There were no running-boards. The mechanical elements were copybook Ford, with a straightforward three-bearing s.v. four-cylinder engine of 1,172 cc, developing 32 b.h.p., and a three-speed synchromesh gearbox. The battery lived under the hood, instead of under the front seat. Brakes were the usual mechanicals, and the car rode on transverse springs, though a low centre of gravity rendered the ride less inacceptable. The Ford was amazing value—£145 ($725) as a four-door sedan, or a good £20 ($100) less than the native product. Despite its three speeds, it was also faster (70 m.p.h.) more frugal (35 m.p.g.) and had better acceleration (0–50 m.p.h. in 18·2 seconds). No wonder more than 96,000 of the first series found buyers between its introduction and the Spring of 1937. The seal was set on Model-C's success when a neat little barrel-sided sporting tourer was offered during 1935. Model-C derivatives were produced in Germany under the 'Eifel' name.

Britons, however, always want more *lebensraum*, and the Model-C, a mere 148 in. long, was a trifle cramped. This was rectified on the 74-series of 1937, which offered external luggage access. Also featured were a dropped and welded frame, pressed-steel wheels and Girling brakes. The new radiator grille had an ecclesiastical air, but unfortunately the latest Ten was higher, heavier and narrower, and handling suffered. So did performance, which was down to an average 62 m.p.h., with acceleration to match. The final manifestation of the basic theme was the Prefect of 1939, basically the 74 with an alligator hood. It was destined for a long run, terminating in 1953 after nearly 380,000 had been built. Even then the old Model-C engine was not dead, for it soldiered on in the sub-utility Popular until 1959.

60 MORRIS TWENTY-FIVE SERIES II, 1936, Great Britain

Morris had no best-seller between 1930 and the Eight of 1935, which explains why their sales were still a beggarly 44,000 in the recovery year of 1933, and why two years later annual

models were discarded in favour of new 'series' introduced as and when the market called for them.

Introduced as a Show surprise in 1932, the original 3½-litre s.v. six-cylinder 25 had sold poorly, probably less than 700 cars in three seasons. The biggest Morris was smooth and well-appointed, but on 60 b.h.p. it was hardly likely to woo Colonials away from their Chevrolets, while its big-bore engine appealed little to tax-conscious Britons—even if for £395 ($1,875) in 1934 they could have synchromesh, hydraulic brakes, a Bendix automatic clutch, a free wheel and all the fashionable gimmicks—fog and spot lamps, a remotely-controlled blind, and interior woodwork in burr walnut.

The Series II Big Sixes introduced in the summer of 1935 represented an attempt to rationalize the range. There were now only two bodies (a sedan and a handsome Special Coupé), and two wheelbase lengths, one for the Sixteen and Eighteen, and the other for the Twenty-One and Twenty-Five. The capacities were 2·1, 2·3, 2·9 and 3·5 litres respectively, and common to all were side valves, four-bearing crankshafts, S.U. downdraught carburetters (made by a Morris subsidiary) and three-speed synchromesh gearboxes. The frames were cruciform-braced, the brakes were the Lockheed hydraulic type standardized on all Morrises since 1934, and the equipment included twin wipers, fog lamps, and built-in jacks. Sedans had built-out, internal-access boots, and the two-tone colour schemes underwent more than one revision during the model's currency. The Series IIs were real bargains, a 25 h.p. *de luxe* sedan selling for only £280. The weight was down by a good 500 pounds, which meant a top speed of 75 m.p.h., with acceleration to match. The redoubtable Humfrey Symons drove a 25 the 6,000 miles from London to Kano (Nigeria) and back, across the Sahara; despite an all-up weight of 2½ tons this Morris would still cruise at 70. 18,391 Series IIs were made, the last ones with monochrome paintwork and pressed-steel wheels. Only the 18 and 25 survived into 1937, and when Morris went over to o.h.v. in 1938, the 25 was the sole survivor of the basic range.

61 MERCEDES-BENZ 170V,
1936, Germany

Daimler-Benz were general suppliers to Germany's middle class during the 1930s' and this activity took precedence over their limited production of exotic, supercharged sporting machinery.

Their s.v. fours and sixes trace their ancestry back to the Stuttgart and Mannheim series of 1928, but with the new decade came more sophisticated chassis: tubular backbones, or, as in the case of the 170V, a cruciform-braced structure built up from oval tubes. All-independent suspension was now standard, with a transverse-leaf arrangement at the front, and swing

axles and coils at the rear; the brakes were hydraulic. This layout made for first-class handling, since swing axles behave admirably if they are not asked to transmit too much power, though there was a tendency to 'hop' over longitudinal corrugations. As economy and durability were the principal objectives, a simple long-stroke s.v. engine of modest output (38 b.h.p. at 3,400 r.p.m.) was used. This had three main bearings, 6-volt coil ignition and gravity feed. The wheelbase was 112 ins.; the car was heavy, at 2,576 pounds, and it needed a good stretch of road to work a 170V up to 70 m.p.h.

Mercedes' earlier utility offerings had been less than successful. The first 170 of 1931 was a gutless and under-geared small six, and the 130H of 1933 was a rear-engined Volkswagen ancestor with tubular backbone frame and a well-substantiated reputation for un-predictable handling. The original 1,308 cc unit was later replaced by the 170V's 1,697 cc motor, but sales were a paltry 10,000 in five seasons. By contrast, the 170V was an excellent if uninspiring machine, competitively priced at RM – 2,350, or less than £250. The Wehrmacht alone took more than 19,000 in various forms, and pre-war production ran to some 70,000 units. If the sedans were stodgy, the open styles, especially the roadsters and two-seater cabriolets, were exceptionally handsome.

After the war the 170V was the first car to go back into production at Stuttgart. Light commercial versions were leaving the works by the autumn of 1946, and sedans nine months later. A total of 49,000 was turned out. Other post-war developments of the theme included the diesel-engined 170D, and the modernized 170S, sold in petrol and diesel forms. These species added another 94,000 units to the score before the old, separate-chassis type was phased out in 1955 in favour of the unitary-construction 180, petrol-powered versions of which were still using the old s.v. engine as late as 1957.

62   OPEL P4, 1936, Germany

Opel had accounted for 68 per cent of all Germany's automobile exports in 1932, and in 1935 they turned out 100,000 cars in a twelvemonth, the first German company to achieve this. Under General Motors' control since 1929, they had come a long way since launching their copy of the 5CV Citroën in 1924.

By 1935 Hitler was reiterating his demands for a People's Car, and already Ferdinand Porsche's official experiments had reached an advanced stage. Opel's approach was, however, that pursued by Ford in Britain; take a conventional and unsophisticated design, reduce frills to a minimum, and make it in such quantities that prices can be progressively cut. Not that they were incapable of *avant-garde* thinking, for already in 1935 they had produced the Olympia, a 1·3-litre s.v. sedan with

unitary construction, Dubonnet-type i.f.s., and headlamps faired into the front wings. This one sold for the equivalent of £125 ($625) in Germany, or for a surprisingly low £155 in England, thanks to state-subsidized exports.

Alongside this interesting machine the P4 of 1936 seemed a retrograde step, since it derived from the 1,016 cc 4/20 of 1929 and the 1·2-litre of 1932. The only modern aspect of the P4 was its short-stroke (67·5 × 75 mm) three-bearing s.v. engine, which gave 23 b.h.p. at 3,660 r.p.m., or fractionally more than the 1·2-litre's more classically-dimensioned, 65 × 90 mm unit. Cooling was by pump, and 6-volt electrics sufficed, though curiously Opel opted for a rear tank and mechanical pump feed at a time when gravity systems were still popular in Germany. Brakes were mechanical, the chassis was an orthodox affair with beam axles at both ends, and the three-speed gearbox (four speeds were an option) had no synchromesh. Buyers had a choice of two two-door bodies, a sedan or a rolltop cabriolet. By 1937 G.M.'s German branch was in the happy position of offering two cheap 1,100 cc models, the P4 and the Kadett, a miniature Olympia on a 92-in. wheelbase for which Germans paid RM—1,795 and Britons little more. At this juncture the price of the P4 was slashed to RM—1,450 or less than £75. This was uncomfortably close to the target of RM—1,240 set for the Volkswagen, and Hitler did not approve. Perhaps it was as well for all concerned that the P4 was not continued into 1939.

63 FIAT 500, 1936, Italy

La Topolino ('Mickey Mouse') was perhaps the most important miniature of the 1930s. The work of Dante Giacosa and Franco Fessia, it was announced in April, 1936, and remained in Fiat's catalogue until the end of 1954. During this period a good half-million were made in Italy, in addition to licence-production by N.S.U. in Germany and Simca in France.

Giovanni Agnelli had planned a 760 cc baby car as early as 1918, but though prototypes were built, he decided that the market was not yet ripe for such devices. His company's 1936 effort remained a true big car in miniature, with four-cylinder, water-cooled engine, a four-speed synchromesh gearbox, independent front suspension and first-rate hydraulic brakes. Better still, Fiat refused to make it anything but a two-seater (the four-seaters produced for the British market in 1939 were built under protest, and not offered anywhere else). A four-seater station wagon only made its appearance in 1948, when a 16·5 b.h.p. o.h.v. engine was adopted for the 500B.

The specification was a simple and orthodox, but liberally drilled, chassis frame with transverse-leaf i.f.s., quarter-elliptic springs at the rear, and the tiny 569 cc short-stroke s.v. engine mounted over the front wheels and ahead of its radiator, an elementary method of warming the passenger compartment. The hood lifted off to give access to the works, the dash-mounted fuel tank incorporated a half-gallon reserve controlled by a tap on the floor, while the two-seater body (either a hardtop or a convertible rolltop) had hollowed-out doors, which gave plenty of elbow-room at the price of awkward, sliding windows. The shape was nicely stream-lined, with recessed door handles and a beetling hood which gave superb forward visibility.

On 13 b.h.p., *La Topolino* was not exactly fast; the two-bearing crank-shaft was apt to protest if 55 m.p.h. were exceeded, and 40 was the comfortable maximum in third. 50 m.p.g. were commonplace, and one early example was driven from Paris to Madrid, averaging 26 m.p.h. and 78 m.p.g. The 128-in. long Mouse could turn in a 28-foot circle, which made it a favourite with housewives, and handling was viceless enough to allow 40 m.p.h. averages on long journeys. The worst basic fault was the smallness of everything, which made certain components only theoretically accessible. It cost £120 ($600) in England, where it had an immense following, so much so that a race was staged for the little creatures at Brooklands in 1938, while in Italy SIATA soon developed an o.h.v. conversion. Highly-tuned editions were raced in Italy as well as in France by Amedée Gordini. By 1940, competition 'Mice' were being persuaded to do 87 m.p.h.

The development from scratch of an out-and-out luxury car of no sporting proclivities was a hazardous undertaking in 1936, yet two British firms attempted it: Rootes with their stillborn straight-eight Sunbeam, and Riley with the Autovia, which actually got into production.

Victor Riley was competing directly against the 25–30 h.p. Rolls-Royce, as can be seen from such ideas as annual inspection schemes, and an Autovia chauffeurs' school. The design was entrusted to Charles van Eugen, formerly of Lea-Francis, and a vee-eight configuration was chosen partly on grounds of compactness, and partly because Riley already offered an engine of this type, the unsuccessful 2·2-litre 8–90. The Autovia unit followed the same lines; the two blocks, set at an angle of 90 degrees, had the bore of the 1½-litre and the stroke of the 9 h.p., and were built in the regular Riley fashion with twin high-set camshafts, hemispherical combustion chambers and detachable heads. Ignition was by magneto, and each bank of cylinders had its own downdraught carburetter and water pump. Fuel feed was by twin electric pumps, and output was a useful 99 b.h.p. This engine was mounted in unit with an automatic clutch and a four-speed preselective gearbox as used on smaller Rileys. The deep-section underslung frame had five cross-members, the worm-drive back axle

was a David Brown product, and the semi-elliptic springs were assisted by hydraulic dampers, with four-position ride control à la Rolls-Royce. Other pleasing touches included one-shot lubrication, built-in jacks and windtone horns. A sports sedan and a limousine were the standard bodies, both by Arthur Mulliner of Northampton. The prices were £975 ($4,875) and £995 ($4,975) respectively.

The prototype appeared in the summer of 1936, but production did not get under way until seven months later. On the road, the Autovia combined an excellent ride with sports-car standards of handling, and even on a weight of 4,500 pounds, a speed of 90 m.p.h. was possible. For 1938 an all-synchromesh gearbox was offered as an option.

Riley's finances were, however, already in a parlous state, and the new Autovia factory remained empty. The thirty-odd vehicles that constituted the total production were put together in the main Riley works. When Lord Nuffield acquired the company in the autumn of 1938, unsold Autovias were quietly remaindered off by a London dealer at £550 each.

65 **RENAULT CELTAQUATRE
8CV**, 1937, France

Renault was as much a general manufacturer as Fiat, since his range usually covered anything from small family sedans to large, rapid and expensive straight-eights. By 1932 the spineless 1½-litre sixes were on their way out, and all cars shamelessly wore their frontal radiators (a 1929 heresy). There was as yet no replacement for the 6CV of the 1920s. A tendency towards bigger cars in France bred in its place a 66 × 95 mm (1·3-litre) 7CV on classic lines, with side valves, coil ignition, thermosyphon circulation, single-plate clutch, wide-ratio three-speed gearbox, and the unhappy combination of semi-elliptic springs at the front and a transverse spring at the rear. The brakes were indifferent, too, but such a perilous set-up mattered little when only 30 b.h.p. were being transmitted to the back axle.

In 1933 the 7CV grew up into a 1,463 cc 8CV (Type YN1), with fan-assisted cooling, synchromesh and rear trunk. Rear tanks and mechanical pumps came with the YN2 of 1934, and during the season the 8CV family evolved into two species, the simple short-chassis Monaquatre (Airsport as Britons knew it), and the first of the Celtaquatres (Airline), a handsome swept-tail sedan with concealed spare wheel, recessed and illuminated rear number plate, and two-toning. 1936 versions had pressed-steel wheels and dashboard change; even on a 104½-in. wheelbase they were six-seaters, while for those in quest of some urge the same basic model could be had with the new 2,383 cc '85' engine.

1937 Renaults had built-out, external boots and ugly vee-grilles in the American idiom. They were cheap and tough; even in England prices started at £189 ($945), and on the home market there was an austerity edition, the Celtastandard. Half the 38,000 Renaults made that year were Celtas, but rigid conservatism was to reap its own reward, Cynical Frenchmen christened the car the '*Salété-Quatre*', as well they might when Peugeots had overhead valves and i.f.s., and Citroën's *tractions* could out-handle all but the best sports cars. Renault were a bad third in home-market sales by 1938, and their only concession to modernity, the 1,003 cc Juvaquatre, took an unconscionable time to reach the public. Less than 30,000 of this crib of the Opel Kadett had been made by the end of 1939, which left the aged Celtaquatre still holding the baby.

66 CADILLAC SIXTY SPECIAL, 1938, USA

Cadillac's vee-eight had become an institution by 1938. Launched in September, 1914, with 5½ litres and 70 b.h.p., it had progressed steadily down the years, with four-wheel brakes in 1924, synchromesh in 1929, and output keeping pace with sophistication and weight. The 1934s, the first to wear i.f.s. (though not, of course, the deplorable 'knees' of lesser General Motors breeds) were followed by 'turret top' bodies in 1935, and by a redesigned range in 1936. These featured brand new cast iron engines with unit block and crankcase, single-plate clutches, hypoid back axles, and hydraulic brakes. Cheaper models ran to 5·3 litres and 125 b.h.p., the 5,676 cc, engine being reserved for the 70 and 75, though it was to be standardized in 1937.

Styling had come full circle. Up to 1927, Cadillacs had been stodgy, but a year later the senior marque fell into line with Harley Earl's La Salle (45), and cars of the 1928–32 period were superbly elegant; their Fleetwood bodies were infinitely superior to the Fisher products used on G.M.'s cheaper lines. Vee-grilles and skirted fenders came in 1933, and gradually what Maurice Hendry has so aptly termed 'cosmetic' touches vanished. 1936 sedans shared their body shells with Buick.

The Sixty Special of 1938 was, however, a style leader following in the wheeltracks of the 1934 La Salle. Mechanical elements were stock: a 5·7-litre engine developing 135 b.h.p., and a three-speed synchromesh gearbox, now endowed with steering-column change, another Cadillac first. The chassis was, however, a new double-drop affair with cruciform bracing, which lowered the vehicle's height by some three inches. The body broke new ground, for it was a four-window sedan on which the boot was truly integral, and not just a stylistic after-thought. The use of thin plated pillars and a vee-screen gave the car a further individuality, and there were no running-boards. If the original version was spoilt by an aggressive horizontal-barred grille, the 1939 edition was more

restrained, although the Buick-type sidemounts were a questionable asset. With a wheelbase of 127 ins. and a list price of $2,090 (£850 in Britain), the Sixty Special was neither the smallest nor the cheapest Cadillac, but it was the one that made the most impression. By 1939 the rest of the range had lost their running-boards, and two years later the influence was plain to see, not only in G.M. products like Buick's Roadmaster and Chevrolet's Fleetline, but in the Studebaker President, and (more indirectly) in Detroit's next styling masterpiece, the Packard Clipper. Before Pearl Harbor, Cadillac's sales were to jump to 66,130 cars in a twelvemonth, and automatic transmission would be a factory option.

67 HUMBER PULLMAN,
1938, Great Britain

As a result of the Depression, many limousine customers deserted the traditional, bespoke, sleeve-valve Daimlers and Minervas in favour of formal carriages based on volume-produced chassis. The fact that these lacked a thoroughbred aura mattered little to owners who never drove, and there was the added advantage of cheap and easy servicing.

The Humber Pullman was a car of this order, which was introduced for 1930 as a prestige, chauffeur-driven edition of the 3,498 cc i.o.e. six-cylinder Snipe. The wheelbase was 130 ins. to the Snipe's 120. The two types developed side-by-side, acquired silent-third gearboxes and downdraught carburetters in 1931, new s.v. engines as part of the Rootes Group's policy of rationalization in 1933, and synchromesh, free wheels, and built-in jacks in 1934. Pullmans became the recognized transport of diplomats, Governor-Generals and Ministers of the Crown. In 1936, King Edward VIII bought one, and the breed was much in evidence at the coronation of his successor, George VI.

For 1936, the six-cylinder Humbers underwent a complete redesign, acquiring new box-girder frame in which the engines sat well forward. The chassis was given transverse-leaf i.f.s., and there was vacuum-servo assistance for the Bendix brakes. Bodies featured integral, flush boots, vee windscreens, and painted radiator shells of traditional Humber shape. New 4·1-litre, four-bearing engines developing 100 b.h.p. were fitted to both Snipe and Pullman. With standard limousine coachwork ('custom' styles were available from Rootes' coachbuilding subsidiary, Thrupp and Maberly), the Pullman weighed just over two tons, and was capable of 75–80 m.p.h.; a gallon of petrol lasted fifteen miles. The price was a modest £735 ($3,675).

The Pullman continued with very little change until 1940, when a razor-edge style of body with projecting boot was introduced, and the brakes were given hydraulic actuation. Though the vast majority of the Humbers used by the Armed Forces

were derivatives of the 'compact' Super Snipe (also with the 4·1-litre engine), Pullmans served as staff cars, and the 1940 model was back in production by late 1945. There was a Pullman in Humber's catalogue until 1954, the last ones using the 4,138 cc pushrod 'Blue Riband' engine.

68 **PEUGEOT 402,** 1938, France.

Peugeot were almost as conservative as Renault, though less addicted to big cars. They were, however, capable of such advanced thinking as transverse i.f.s. and twin *bloctube* frames on the stolid 201 and 301 models of 1932. These, along with worm drive, another Peugeot characteristic, were to feature on their 1936 models, but it was the looks that were revolutionary.

The 402 conformed to prevailing French ideas on middle-class family sedans. It had a big, lazy, 56 b.h.p. 2-litre four-cylinder engine, now with o.h.v., Peugeot's first such deviation for some years. The standard gearbox was of three-speed synchromesh type, and in long-chassis form the car measured 130 ins. between wheel centres, an ideal length for an eight-seater *familiale*. Adequate power made for a civilized top-gear ratio of 4·6:1, a welcome change from the abysmal gearing of their earlier seven-passenger machines. Brakes were mechanical, and the cantilever rear springs gave a good ride. Futher, the 402 was streamlined, with a short beetling hood of the type recently adopted by Fiat. But where the Fiat (and most of its contemporaries) hid its headlamps in the wings, the Peugeot's were tucked away between grille and radiator proper, a location shared by the battery.

A wide range of 402s was offered, including light commercials, an 'electric coupé' (or convertible with power-operated, disappearing *steel* top), and even a sports model, the 402DS with 70 b.h.p. engine and wind-down retractable windscreen, which was good for 80–85 m.p.h. All passenger models were available to order with a four-speed electrically-selected gearbox incorporating an overdrive top, and for family motorists in a hurry there was the 402 *Légère*, a hybrid combining the 402 engine with the chassis and body of the smaller 1·7-litre 302.

By 1939, 402s had been given new 83 × 99 mm (2,142 cc) power units developing 63 b.h.p. They also had the curious Michelin Pilote wheels with 'starfish' spokes as found on contemporary Citroëns, while Peugeot were selling the big sedan bodies to Berliet for *their* 11CV. A total of 58,748 402s (including some three thousand taxis) were made up to the end of 1941.

69 AERO A30, A50,
Czechoslovakia, 1938

Dr Kabes's aircraft firm entered the motor industry in 1929 with a simple unitary-construction cyclecar powered by a 494 cc single-cylinder water-cooled two-stroke engine. This transmitted its 10 b.h.p. to a back axle without differential through the medium of a cone clutch and a three-speed gearbox. There were no front-wheel brakes, and one paid extra for a starter; the standard equipment was a rope device with dashboard 'control'! This light-weight had grown up by 1932 into a more sophisticated 662 cc twin with f.w.b.: Aero's production that year was 1,317 units. It was, however, the 1934 type that was to make the most impression. The work of Ing. Busek, these front-wheel drive cars used all-independently-sprung platform frames, with mechanical brakes and friction dampers. As before, engines were two-strokes and water-cooled (by pump and fan) but unlike contemporary D.K.W.s, the Aero had deflector-type pistons of light alloy. Another vital difference between the German and Czechoslovak designs was that Aero's engines were always longitudinally mounted. The 999 cc twin-cylinder A30 developed 20 b.h.p. at 3,500 r.p.m.; the A50 was a four of exactly double the capacity giving 48 b.h.p. Such features as alloy cylinder heads, 6-volt coil ignition, and gravity feed were common to both species. So were the bodies, which were low-built and good-looking in a curiously 'English' way. A low hood line had its snags, for the battery was mounted in the engine compartment in such a position that a wheel had to be removed to get it out. The ratios of the Aero's three-speed gearbox were selected by the usual clumsy lever on the dash.

An A50 sedan weighed 2,325 pounds and was capable of 75 m.p.h., though it proved less smooth than the twin, and suffered from strong oversteer on full power. Aero's annual sales in the later 1930s were around a thousand cars; some were sold abroad, mainly to the Baltic States, Hungary and Rumania.

After the War, Czechoslovakia's automobile industry was nationalized, but even before this step was taken, production had been concentrated on the Aero Minor (a Jawa-based two-stroke owing nothing to Busek's Aeros), the 1,100 cc Skoda (70) and the rear-engined Tatras. The Aero A30 was, however, briefly revived, and a small number of cars with redesigned grilles were produced between 1946 and 1948.

70 SKODA POPULAR 1100, 1938, Czechoslovakia

Czechoslovakia's biggest car makers were (and are) Skoda, an armaments firm who took over Laurin-Klement's Mlada Boleslav works in 1925. Early Skodas were American in concept and conventional in specification, as well as being produced in all manner of sizes. In 1934, however, the company took a big step forward by marketing a modern light car, the 995 cc s.v. four-cylinder 420, with forked backbone frame, all-independent suspension (by transverse leaf at the front and swing axles at the rear), and a three-speed

synchromesh gearbox. This evolved into the first Popular, a simpler affair with 903 cc and 18 b.h.p., not to mention a gearbox mounted in unit with the differential-less back end. Ignition was by 6-volt coil, cooling by thermosyphon, and synchromesh was not provided. Top speed was 55 m.p.h., with a fuel consumption of 32 m.p.g. These early Populars were subjected to intensive testing; one car was driven overland from Czechoslovakia to India, while others undertook tours of Africa, and Northern and Central America. A Skoda finished eighth in the 1936 Monte Carlo Rally.

Experiments with rear-engined light cars in the Ganz idiom were not followed up, but 995 cc o.h.v. engines, rated at 27 b.h.p., came in 1937, when differentials were provided. The steering was by rack-and-pinion, though brakes were still mechanical, and bodies had a certain elegance, especially the roadsters and the rare fastback coupés. By the end of the year a pump-cooled model was available for use in hot countries, while Skoda began to look westwards, exporting some cars to France. 1938 saw the first of the redesigned 1,089 cc, 32 b.h.p. engines with three main bearings and wet liners, the first four-speed gearboxes made their appearance, and bodies were appreciably wider.

Production of the 1100 was resumed in 1946, the main changes being the standardization of hydraulic brakes and a new, stylized front-end treatment. Descendants of this 1101 were the 440

(Octavia) series introduced in 1954, which were still being produced in van and station-wagon forms in December, 1971.

71 CROSLEY, 1939, 1940, USA

'Why Build a Battleship to Cross a River', was the slogan of Powel Crosley, Jr., a radio manufacturer and small-car enthusiast. Undeterred by the sad fate of the American Austin Seven (launched in 1930 to the accompaniment of much ballyhoo and alleged firm orders for 52,000 cars, only to land in receivership four years later after selling less than 20,000), he elected to market a minicar in 1939.

Like Fiat (63) he planned his light-weight strictly as a two-seater with plenty of legroom for tall people. Power came from an oversquare air-cooled flat-twin 655 cc Waukesha engine rated at 12·5 b.h.p., and the other mechanical elements were equally simple – a three-speed gearbox, single dry-plate clutch, and spiral bevel rear axle. Rear suspension was quarter-elliptic, and interesting barbarities included the absence of a fuel gauge (a graduated dipstick was affixed to the filler cap), the omission of any universal joints from the propeller shaft, and brake linings which were not riveted to the shoes, but 'floated'. The hand brake 'lever' was a pull-up chain which locked itself into a groove for parking!

The Crosley measured ten feet from stem to stern, turned the scales at 925 pounds, and sold for $325 (£65), or $330 complete with radio (by Crosley, of course). This was at a time when Ford's prices started at $599, and Chevrolet's at $628. The recently resuscitated Bantam (née American Austin) cost $399. By 1941, four-seater Crosleys were available, capacity was down to 580 cc, and the necessity for universal joints had been recognized.

Unfortunately, the demand for 'cute' small cars—the Fiat 500 was currently the USA's best-selling foreign import, though on sales of 400 a year it scarcely helped Italy's foreign-exchange problems—soon wore off, and the first season's deliveries of 1,161 units represented Crosley's best pre-war showing. None the less, the little car functioned adequately. One early owner had to pay $850 for his 1941 four-seater, thanks to wartime shortages, but extracted 31,000 miles of trouble-free motoring from the vehicle. 'Hairy' roadholding and a rough engine limited the comfortable cruising speed to 40 m.p.h., but it could cope with a full complement of passengers, and was persuaded on occasion to do 60 m.p.h.

After the War Crosley moved on to bigger o.h.c. fours, selling over 25,000 in 1948, his banner year. The *marque* died in 1952.

72 STANDARD FLYING 8, 1939, Great Britain

Standard, later to become the 'sick man' of the British motor industry, had gone from strength to strength under J. P. Black in the 1930s. They consolidated their position in 1936 with the fastback Flying Standard family designed by E. G. Grinham. Initially limited to the top end of the range, these designs had spread by 1937 to embrace everything from a 1,131 cc Nine (which sold well) to an interesting 'compact' 2·7-litre vee-eight (which did not). That year's deliveries of 40,000 cars were Standard's best to date.

What the company lacked, however, was a contender in the 8 h.p. class to rival Austin, Morris and Ford, and this was announced in September, 1938 with much fanfare, as 'The Car To Beat the Budget'. All this really implied was that Standard had adopted the classical, long-stroke dimensions of 57 × 100 mm for their engine, though there was a lot more to the Eight. Its s.v. engine was more powerful (31 b.h.p. at 4,000 r.p.m.) than any of its competitors; though as yet made only in two-door form, the car was roomy and had an external-access boot. It was also the first native Eight with independent front springing. Cooling was by thermosyphon; like Ford, Standard were content with three speeds (there was, of course, synchromesh on the upper two) and 6-volt electrics. Brakes were the unpredictable Bendix, but the lever, of umbrella-handle type, worked on all four wheels. In view of the success of the open Morris Eights, Standard wisely included a tourer in the range, undercutting the Morris at £125 ($625). A pretty miniature drop-head coupé joined the line-up during the season, and a four-door sedan was announced in 1940, though very few of these last were made.

The new Standard gave 60 m.p.h. and 45 m.p.g. It was an instant success, 10,000 finding buyers in the first five months. The model was reinstated in 1945 with four forward speeds, by which time post-war inflation had pushed the price up to £313. A one-model policy was to bring about the Eight's demise in 1948. The 83,139th and last rolled off the lines that July; it was presented to the company's oldest employee, Albert Smith, in recognition of his 43 years' service.

73 **AMILCAR COMPOUND**
   B38, 1939, France

Unlike Salmson, Amilcar had not prospered after their switch from small sports cars to bigger and less sporting machinery. Their 2½-litre sports 'Pégase' was a temperamental brute and its touring counterpart, the 12CV with o.h.v. Delahaye engine and Cotal gearbox, was hardly competitive. By 1937 they were dependent on financial help from Hotchkiss, with whose backing they launched an ingenious f.w.d. light car from the drawing-board of J. A. Grégoire.

This machine (always a Hotchkiss-Amilcar in England) had unitary construction with a difference, since the side-members, both sills, front cross-member, firewall and screen pillars were all of Alpax, a light alloy. The 1,185 cc s.v. four-cylinder Amilcar engine drove forward to a four-speed gearbox, from where the drive was taken back to a spiral bevel unit of Tracta type. Steering was by rack and pinion. The brakes were cable-operated, and all four wheels were independently sprung, by two superimposed transverse springs at the front and by torsion bars at the back. Despite a modest weight of 1,848 lbs, the B38 was not particularly brisk, and called for liberal use of the gear lever, an unpleasing dashboard-mounted affair with a cable linkage running over the top of the engine.

Like many an advanced design, the B38 took a long time to reach the public. A prototype was successfully driven from Paris to Baghdad and then to London in the summer of 1938, but no cars were actually delivered before 1939, and only 681 had been produced before the Fall of France brought the story to an end. The range included a cabriolet and a roadster as well as the regular two-door sedan. In April 1940, a successor was ready in the shape of the B67 with 1,340 cc, 45 b.h.p. o.h.v. engine, but this never saw production. Plans for the Amilcar's revival in 1946 were frustrated by the loss of all jigs and drawings during the Occupation, though Grégoire went on to apply his structural ideas to the ingenious flat-twin Dyna-Panhard, as well as to a bigger, 2-litre flat-four which Hotchkiss eventually marketed at great expense to themselves. Another Amilcar derivative was the Belgian Imperia TA8 of 1947, which used the B67 engine,

though its three-speed gearbox and composite wood-and-metal body were legacies from the Adlers which Imperia had built under licence between 1934 and 1940.

74 CITROËN 15CV, 1939, France

Citroën's first front-wheel drive car, the 1,300 cc o.h.v. 7CV, came out in 1934. It proved the last straw for André Citroën's over-extended finances, though thanks to a rescue operation by Michelin the car's teething troubles were overcome. By 1938 Citroën's fortunes were riding high; the *traction* was France's best-selling car, with 61,640 units delivered—9,000 more than Peugeot, and a cool 18,000 more than Renault.

As yet, however, their biggest model was the long-chassis 11CV, an eight-seater version of the 1,911 cc four. A 22CV vee-eight using a brace of 11CV blocks had been exhibited at the 1934 Salon, but never followed up; even the prototypes did their trials with Ford V8 motors under their hoods.

By October, 1938, the gap had been bridged with the new 15CV six. Structurally it followed the *traction*'s successful formula of full unitary construction with a flat, welded floor; the engine and drive unit were bolted to the front horns. Torsion-bar suspension was used all round, and the three-speed synchromesh gearbox lived out front, with the drive taken back through primary and secondary shafts to the bevel pinion.

The wet-liner o.h.v. engines were fed by mechanical pump, the brakes were hydraulic, and later cars had excellent rack-and-pinion steering. The inevitable dashboard gear-change was no worse than others of its kind.

The result was an astonishingly stable car with a low centre of gravity, capable of putting up commendable averages on very modest outputs, and endowed with immense structural strength. Its faults were excessive length, heavy steering at low speeds, a poor turning circle (the 15CV required 46 feet), acute rust-proneness, and complicated maintenance schedules—beyond the average small garage, let alone the home mechanic.

The Six was a scaled-up 11CV with four-bearing 2,866 cc engine developing a useful 76 b.h.p. The other differences of design were the vertical shock absorbers at the front, a more compact gearbox with shorter drive shafts, and torque-resistant dampers which could be troublesome, causing outbursts of transmission snatch. The 15CV was very long—191 inches overall—and no car for a woman. It was, however, capable of an easy 80 m.p.h., and soon became a favourite with bank robbers.

Only 2,000 were made before the War, but another 48,000 were produced between 1945 and 1955, including some Chapron-bodied presidential carriages. By this time, of course, the *quinze* was profiting from the fearsome imposts imposed by the Government on cars of higher taxable horsepower. The last models were available with an early edition of the *Déesse*'s hydro-pneumatic suspension, although at the rear only.

75 HORCH 930, 1939, Germany

Apart from a short-lived 6-litre V-12 of 1931–33, Horch made nothing but eights between 1926 and 1939. From 1933, however, the expensive straight-eight at RM—12,500 (£625) was joined by a more modest 3-litre vee-eight retailing at RM—8,250. This one had side valves, the blocks were set at an angle of 60 degrees, and the specification embraced a dual-choke down-draught carburetter fed by mechnical pump, 12-volt coil ignition, and pump cooling. The four-speed gearbox had synchromesh on its three upper ratios, and initially duo-servo mechanical brakes were specified; hydraulics made their appearance very early on.

First of this complicated range—Horch changed their model designations with disconcerting frequency—was the 830, with 2,984 cc, 60 b.h.p. engine in a 126-inch wheelbase, but by 1935 capacity was up to 3¼ litres with the 830B. This soon gave way to the 3,517 cc 830BK and 830BL, the latter on a 131-inch chassis with independent front suspension. Jointed-axle rear springing of semi-independent type had been available since 1935, but both types of eight were still found with beam axles at both ends as late as 1939. The last of the family were the 930V and 930BL (1939–40) with 3·8 litres, jointed-axle rear ends, twin horizontal Solex carburetters, and one-shot lubrication. The long-chassis version was also catalogued as an ambulance.

In 1939 form, the vee-eight Horch could cruise at a comfortable 75-80 m.p.h. in overdrive. Like Adler, B.M.W. and Hansa, Auto Union were playing with an aerodynamic *autobahn*-cruiser designed to take advantage of Germany's new road system. High gearing and a perfect shape compensated for the lack of brute force. The Horch version appeared at the 1939 Berlin Show, and was as ugly as the others, the thickness of one front wing concealing a wash-basin, while the seats converted into a bed. Top speed was quoted as 95 m.p.h., but there was no production. Horch vee-eights were badly needed for other purposes, the car being the Wehrmacht's equivalent of the Humber Super Snipe. Since 1933, it had been supplied in all manner of forms, with open *Kübelwagen*, van or station wagon bodywork, not to mention heavy 4 × 4 versions. Generals like Guderian and Rommel rode in them. Another service customer was the Spanish Falangist Air Force, whose last Horchs were not finally pensioned off until the 1960s.

76 VOLKSWAGEN, 1939,
Germany

For all the dubious politics surrounding it, the *Kraft durch Friede* (Strength Through Joy) car was a *fait accompli* by

1939, and was ready for series production, had not the Third Reich been preoccupied with weightier matters. The unrealistic price of 900 *reichsmarks* (or even the 1,240 which were probably nearer the truth), the monumental savings-stamp scheme which raised 289 million marks in weekly contributions, and the vast Wolfsburg plant which never worked at more than 25 per cent capacity should not blind anyone to the recognition that Hitler was right in his beliefs. A demand *did* exist for a simple vehicle capable of cruising at 100 km/h (62 m.p.h.) under *autobahn* conditions. The Führer did not, of course, live to see his dream-car beat Model-T's record of 15,007,033 units, an objective attained by the Beetle in February, 1972.

The genesis of the VW goes back to the Hanomag (12) and to Josef Ganz's experimental small cars with forked-backbone frames, built by Ardie and Adler in 1930-31. The first official prototype was Ferdinand Porsche's Project 12, a Tatra-styled device with rear-mounted 1·2-litre water-cooled radial engine, built by Zündapp in 1933. Next came another Porsche creation, N.S.U.'s Volksauto, which introduced an o.h.v. 1½-litre flat-four engine of oversquare (80 × 72 mm) dimensions, as well as torsion-bar springing all round. During the next few years Puch twin-piston two-stroke units were tried and discarded, as were the hydraulic brakes of the Zündapp and N.S.U. cars; air cooling, however, had come to stay. By 1937 the Volkswagen as we now know it had taken shape, even though prototypes of that period suffered from the same total lack of rearward vision as afflicted the big Tatra (55).

None of the 1939 models, of course, reached a subscriber, and in fact only 210 civilian versions were actually built under the Hitler *régime*. But all the essential elements of success were there; a 986 cc engine with turbo-fan cooling, a platform frame, all-round torsion-bar springing, built-in ventilation, and the unmistakable shape, though the rear window was still of divided type. Main technical differences between ancient and modern were the mechanical brakes (still a feature of basic models as late as 1962) and the absence of synchromesh (which did not become compulsory until the end of 1964). The sole beneficiaries of all this ingenuity were as yet the Wehrmacht, who used thousands of 4 × 2 *Kübelwagen*, not to mention its amphibious derivatives. The post-War 1,131 cc engine was in fact introduced in March, 1943.

77 ZIS-101, 1939, USSR

The Russian automobile industry had never amounted to much, even in Imperial days, and in any case trucks were the first priority for the new *régime*. Before 1930, no private cars were produced in series, and even with Ford assistance the immense Molotov Works at Gorki got away to a shaky start. During the whole of 1931, its production amounted to fifteen GAZ-As, or thinly-disguised Model-A Fords; in 1935, the first year for which detailed statistics are available, Russia turned out a paltry 5,987 passenger cars.

The GAZ-A and its descendants fulfilled utilitarian needs, but it would never do for the Party *élite* to ride around in Packards and Lincolns. So arose the ZIS series, of which prototypes were constructed in the Krasny Putilovjets factory, though production was entrusted to Moscow's *Zavod Imieni Stalin* (Stalin Automobile Works) at Moscow. Only eight examples of the original ZIS-100 were built; this was a carbon copy of the 1932 Buick Limited, powered by a 115 b.h.p. o.h.v. straight-eight engine with a capacity of 5,650 cc. Servo brakes were fitted. The series-produced 101 of 1936 was also Buick under the hood, despite a marked resemblance, especially at the front end, to the 1935 Airstream Chrysler. The three-speed synchromesh gearbox followed accepted American lines, but G.M.'s new i.f.s. was not used. Thanks to a strictly limited 'market' (the ZIS was a badge of rank and not on sale anywhere), production costs were murderously high, reputedly $75,000 (£15,000) per car! Engines were made with cast-iron or alloy pistons, respective outputs being 90 and 115 b.h.p.

By 1939 the 101 had downdraught carburation, and cars were produced with limousine or tourer bodies; one of the former, imported by Ambassador Ivan Maisky, was the first Russian automobile to be registered in Britain. During the last two years of peace ZIS also made the 102 tourer. Capacity was unchanged, but the twin-plate clutch and power brakes were new. Once again the styling was based on Chrysler, with a grille modelled on that of the 1938 Imperial Eight.

After the War, of course, ZIS profited from a deal born of the Grand Alliance, in which Packard sold all their 'Senior' body dies to the Soviet Government. The resultant ZIS-110 was a convincing and well-made replica of the Packard 180, and a much better-looking effort than any of the peculiar shapes affected by the American concern in its declining years.

78 HILLMAN MINX, 1940, Great Britain

The Hillman Minx was one of Britain's few 1940 models to go straight into production, thanks to Service orders. Along with the Austin (46), the 1,185 cc s.v. Hillman had spearheaded a new generation of Family Tens, which replaced the Twelves of the 1920s. The three-bearing engine, with mechanical pump feed and 6-volt coil ignition, developed 30 b.h.p., and rode on 'cushioned power' rubber mountings. The single-plate clutch, three-speed unit gearbox with central change, semi-elliptic suspension and Bendix brakes were to be expected. By 1933, the model's second season, a wide range of coachwork was available, though a basic sedan could be bought for less than £160 ($800), and during the

season four forward speeds made their appearance. Subsequent Minx evolution followed prevailing British fashion; lockable free wheels in 1934, and 'variload' springs and draughtless ventilation in 1935, when Hillman adopted an all-synchromesh box (abandoned for economy reasons four years later), and catalogued, briefly, a de luxe sedan with factory-installed radio. A complete redesign for 1936 transformed the Minx into a fastback with internal-access boot, pressed-steel wheels, a stronger, box-girder frame, and down-draught carburation. Output rose to 33 b.h.p., and the car was bigger and roomier. Thereafter minor changes carried the model through to 1939, by which time only sedans, a drophead coupé, and a station wagon (marketed under the Commer name) were offered.

The 1940 series, however, was a major step forward, since the separate chassis was eliminated in favour of full unitary construction. Body shape was little changed apart from the built-out boot, but behind a revised grille lay an alligator-type hood. Provision was made for a radio; the piston type dampers were a legacy from 1939, but for the first time 12-volt electrics were used. 112 pounds of weight were saved by the new structure, and certainly the new Minx was good for 65 m.p.h. and 30 m.p.g., though handling remained indifferent. Serious civilian production, of course, would not get under way until 1945, but during the War a small number of sedans to 'service' specification (no chromium plating, small-diameter headlamps, and black paintwork) were turned out for essential users such as doctors.

79 CHEVROLET SPECIAL DE LUXE SERIES-AH, 1941, USA

By the late 1930s Chevrolet's 'Cast Iron Wonder', the legendary o.h.v. six introduced in 1929, had become America's Universal Car, as well as holding a commanding position in export markets where taxation did not rule out a 3½-litre engine or a 20 m.p.g. thirst. The company's sales finally passed Ford's in 1931, and with one exception (1935) Chevrolet never lost the lead again before Pearl Harbor. A steady 25 per cent share of the home market was a tribute to a simple pressure-and-splash lubricated power unit which lent itself to 'flat-rate' servicing.

Capacity and power went up, from 3·2 litres and 46 b.h.p. in 1929 to 3½ litres and 90 b.h.p. in 1941. Weight also increased (but not alarmingly) by a mere 200 pounds in thirteen seasons. The cars acquired synchromesh in 1932, no-draught ventilation in 1933, optional 'Knee Action' i.f.s. in 1934, 'turret top' styling in 1935 and hydraulic brakes in 1936. In 1937, the Chevrolet was completely redesigned, with a box-girder frame, a hypoid rear axle, and a new, enlarged four-bearing engine. By 1940 the influence of Cadillac's Sixty Special (66) was apparent. The hood was of forward-opening type, the grille was a grille and not a stylized radiator, running-boards had all but vanished, and all models had column change. A year later the beam-axle option (aimed at conservative customers who had found the alarming ways of the old 'knees' not to their liking) had gone, and the Chevrolet had assumed the basic shape it was to keep until 1948. Headlamps disappeared into the front wings, a heavy, three-piece chromium-plated grille dominated the front end, and a vee windscreen was provided. 'Special *De Luxe*' variants were distinguishable by their stainless steel mouldings, horn rings on the steering-wheel and armrests on the front doors, while body styles included a power-top convertible and a timbered station wagon of the type popularized by Ford in the middle thirties. During the season came two further models, a four-window sport sedan on Sixty Special lines, and the Aerosedan, a two-door six-seater fastback coupé of a type which General Motors-Holdens, the group's Australian offshoot, had been making for local consumption since 1935. So when Chevrolet went to War, the Division was sitting pretty, with model-year sales of well over a million. Calendar-year sales were 930,293, or 330,000 more than Ford, and more than double Plymouth's figures. As for the Cast Iron Wonder, it had eight post-war years ahead of it, though the last cars it would power were to differ substantially from the 1941s.

Among the American industry's also-rans were Nash. Committed to the competitive middle-class market (apart from occasional sallies into carriage trade and bargain basement alike), they struggled through the difficult thirties on good management rather than impressive sales. Their best performance was 85,949 units in 1937, and their best national placing tenth. Their principal gimmicks were the dual-ignition o.h.v. engines of their costlier models, and their 'Weather Eye' air conditioning of 1938. Since 1934 they had tried hard with a series of cheap L-head sixes in the $700–900 ($140–180) bracket, initially under the name of La Fayette. The 600 of 1941 was, however, something new.

Neither in appearance nor in basic specification was the car very interesting. The 2·8-litre six-cylinder engine, a four-bearing s.v. affair developing 75 b.h.p. at 3,600 r.p.m., was on the small side, and in an era of elongated seventeen-footers, the car looked a real compact on its 112-in. wheelbase. Mechanical pump feed was to be expected, the three-speed synchromesh gearbox had column change and the brakes were, of course, hydraulic. Air conditioning and overdrive were standard Nash extras, and the six-window sedans (made in 'sweptback' or 'trunk-back' shapes) were often seen in the fashionable two-tone finishes. Nash might claim that the all-coil suspension (with a beam axle at the rear) gave a 'new kind of ride', but Buick owners, who had been enduring such a set-up since 1938, might not agree. The car was exceptionally light, at 2,615 pounds, and its 25 m.p.g. thirst was appreciated with petrol rationing looming close. The sedan price of $815 ($163) made it slightly more expensive than a Chevrolet.

What made it different was its full unitary construction, in which a box-section frame was welded direct to the body, the first instance of such a technique being applied to a really cheap American car.

The model was to return after 1945, but it was not until 1950 that Nash at last hit the jackpot with the first of their Ramblers, a roll-top, slab-sided convertible measuring only 174 inches from stem to stern, and capable of 80 m.p.h. Within nine years it would push the company (now merged with Hudson to form American Motors) into fourth place in home sales, kill off the Nash name, and frighten the Big Three into a crash programme of smaller cars. Whether Americans knew it or not in 1941, the seeds of the compact proper had been sown.

INDEX

Make	*Model*	*Ref. No.* (*colour*)	*Page No.* (*description*)
Aero	A30, A50	69	158
Amilcar	Compound B38	73	161
Austin	Ten-Four	46	137
Autovia	24 h.p.	64	154
Bean	Fourteen	3	98
Berliet	11CV	23	116
Beverley-Barnes	24–80 h.p.	10	105
Bianchi	S4	14	108
B.M.W.	Dixi 3/15PS	34	126
Buick	Series–40	57	147
Cadillac	Sixty Special	66	155
Chevrolet	Special De Luxe Series–AH	79	167
Chrysler	CD	36	128
Citröen	15CV	74	162
Clyno	10·8 h.p.	16	110
Crosley	1939, 1940	71	160
Custom	Supercharger Eight	44	135
Dagmar	24–6–80	1	97
Daimler	Double-Six-50	20	114
Datsun	1935, 1937	56	146
De Soto	Airflow SE	52	143
De Vaux	6–75	37	129
D.K.W.	F1–500	40	131
Erskine	Six	18	112
Farman	A6B 40CV	6	101
Fiat	500	63	153
F.N.	1625	35	127
Ford	Ten	59	149
Ford	V8 model–18	43	134
Franklin	Series 17	50	141
Goliath	Dreiradwagen	48	139
Gräf *und* Stift	SP8	42	133
Graham	Blue Streak	44	135

Make	Model	Ref. No. (colour)	Page No. (description)
Hanomag	'Komissbrot' 2/10PS	12	107
Hillman	Minx	78	166
Horch	930	75	163
Hotchkiss	AM2 12CV	21	115
Humber	Pullman	67	156
Imperia	6CV	25	118
J.M.B.	1934, 1935	53	144
Jowett	Long Four	4	99
La Licorne	5CV	28	121
Lancia	Augusta	51	142
La Salle	1932, 1934	45	136
Lincoln–Zephyr	1936, 1937	58	148
Locomobile	Junior Eight	9	104
Magosix	1929	30	123
Martini	NF	41	132
Mathis	PS 10CV	7	102
Maybach	W3, W5	13	107
Mercedes–Benz	170V	61	151
Minerva	AP 22CV	49	140
Morris	Twenty-Five Series II	60	150
N.A.G.	D4	8	103
Nash	600	80	168
Oakland	6–54	2	98
Opel	P4	62	154
Overland	Whipper Four	15	109
Packard	Super Eight	19	113
Panhard	6CS 13CV	47	138
Peugeot	402	68	157
Pierce-Arrow	Eight	32	124
Praga	Alfa	29	122
Renault	Celtaquatre 8CV	65	154
Rolls Royce	Twenty	5	100
Roosevelt	1929	26	119
Rover	14 h.p.	54	144

Make	Model	Ref. No. (colour)	Page No. (description)
Salmson	S4	33	125
Sima-Violet	1925	11	106
Singer	Junior	22	116
Skoda	Popular 1100	70	159
Standard	Flying 8	72	160
Star	Comet Eighteen	38	130
Steyr	Type XII	17	111
Stoewer	S10 Superior, G15 Gigant	24	117
Swift	10 h.p.	27	120
Tatra	77	55	145
Triumph	Scorpion	39	131
Volkswagen	1939	76	164
Volvo	PV651, PV653	31	123
ZIS–101	1939	77	165